#In Purpose In Practice
JOURNAL

A Six Month Practice Journal
for Musicians

Dear Practicer,

Thank you for joining me in a renewed commitment to practicing well! This practice journal came from a desire to help each of you accomplish your biggest goals as musicians. I want you all to learn the secrets and joys of practicing consistently, efficiently, and purposefully! Inside you'll find all the ingredients to a successful practice session: Weekly and daily practice logs, inspirational quotes, all my favorite practice techniques and lots of space to reflect.

This journal will get you through six months of daily practice! At the beginning of each week, a practice tip appears. As you progress to each new week, take each new practice tip to heart and add it to your toolbox. My practice companion handbook, *Purpose In Practice: 26 Rules for the Practicing Musician,* explains each of those practice tips in detail, with practical steps toward mastering each one. If you work towards mastering all of these tips, you should be a professional practicer by the end of your six months!

As you practice, I would love to hear from you! Please take the time to write a review, send me an Instagram DM @rachelleehall, and post your practice videos to *#PurposeInPractice* so our Instagram community can share in your practicing experience!

My hope with this book is that it will help you pursue meaning in every practice session–because if you practice with purpose, there is great *#PurposeInPractice.*

Happy practicing!

Rachel Lee Hall

S.D.G.

Welcome to the
#PurposeInPractice Journal!

Here is a step-by-step guide to making sure you get the most benefit
out of this practice journal. Let's get started!

Practice Tips To Begin The Week

At the beginning of each week, the first thing you'll see is a brand new practice tip. Use this as a strategy for the week to add to your practicing arsenal! Feel free to use this page however you like. Bring it to life with colored pencils (markers might bleed through the page) on your rest day. Scan it and tape it up to your wall for motivation. IG it to inspire all your friends (using the #PurposeInPractice hashtag!). Anything that will help you improve your game.

Your Week At A Glance

Next, you'll find your weekly spread. This is your place to put down your week-long goals, pencil in any deadlines, put down gigs, rehearsals, lessons, and performance dates. It gives you a vision of your week at a glance so you can collect all your goals into one place.

Reflection

Your rest day is a great time to reflect on the week. What went well? What can you do better? It's important to process your practice time and figure out how to refine it in order to be even more productive and efficient. Jot down the repertoire you worked through and any special sections or measures you feel proud of conquering! There is also space for lesson notes. If you don't have a music teacher, use this space to reflect on lessons you have learned for yourself this week.

Journal Pages

There are two practice days per page, for a total of six practice days per week and one rest day. Yes, I know it's countercultural to advocate for a rest day as a classical musician. But you can read all about that in my handbook!

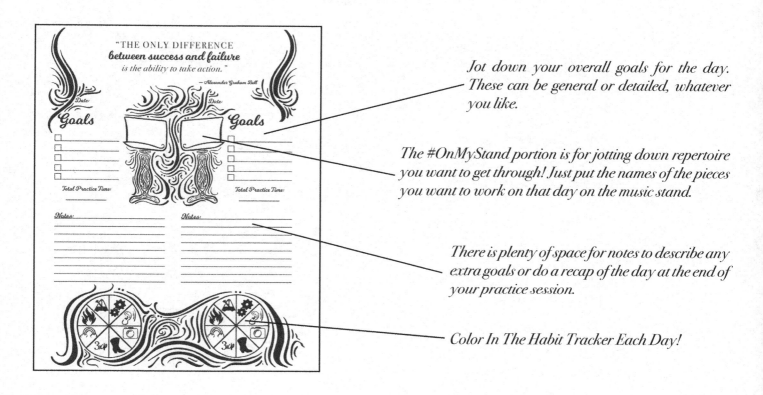

Jot down your overall goals for the day. These can be general or detailed, whatever you like.

The #OnMyStand portion is for jotting down repertoire you want to get through! Just put the names of the pieces you want to work on that day on the music stand.

There is plenty of space for notes to describe any extra goals or do a recap of the day at the end of your practice session.

Color In The Habit Tracker Each Day!

The Habit Tracker

These are eight things that I found to be the most important secrets to a great practice session!
Use colored pencils to shade in each pie slice each day if you complete:

 Warm Up
Scales/arpeggios/etudes/whatever your typical warm-up routine might be!

 Boot Camp
Play at least one section slowly at a single volume. Read more about this in my handbook!

 Listen To Music
Bonus points if it helps you understand your current repertoire

 Technique
Improve at least one aspect of your technique today.

 Dynamics & Expression
Practice dynamics, phrasing and musical expression.

 Metronome
Did you use your metronome today?

 #3XPerfectly Rule
Commit to doing a small passage three times perfectly before moving on or upping the tempo. If you mess up on the second time you have to start over!

 Record Yourself
Record yourself and play it back to get a new perspective. Don't forget to post your progress to #PurposeInPractice on Instagram!

Be Willing to Do Whatever it Takes

A worthy purpose cultivates worthy practice.

IF YOUR PURPOSE IS WORTHY ENOUGH, YOU WILL BE WILLING TO DO WHATEVER IT TAKES TO ACCOMPLISH IT.

Your Week
At A Glance

MONDAY

TUESDAY

WEDNESDAY

THURSDAY

Goals
for the week

- [ ] _____
- [ ] _____
- [ ] _____
- [ ] _____
- [ ] _____
- [ ] _____
- [ ] _____
- [ ] _____
- [ ] _____
- [ ] _____
- [ ] _____
- [ ] _____
- [ ] _____
- [ ] _____
- [ ] _____

FRIDAY

SATURDAY

SUNDAY

"There is no merit in just thinking about doing something.
The result is exactly the same as not thinking about it.
IT IS ONLY DOING THE THING THAT COUNTS."

— *Schiniki Suzuki*

Date:

Goals

- ☐ _____
- ☐ _____
- ☐ _____
- ☐ _____
- ☐ _____

Total Practice Time:

_____

Date:

Goals

- ☐ _____
- ☐ _____
- ☐ _____
- ☐ _____
- ☐ _____

Total Practice Time:

_____

Notes: _____

_____
_____
_____
_____
_____
_____
_____
_____

Notes: _____

_____
_____
_____
_____
_____
_____
_____
_____

Date:

Goals

- [ ]
- [ ]
- [ ]
- [ ]
- [ ]

Total Practice Time:
_____

Notes:
_____
_____
_____
_____
_____
_____
_____
_____

Date:

Goals

- [ ]
- [ ]
- [ ]
- [ ]
- [ ]

Total Practice Time:
_____

Notes:
_____
_____
_____
_____
_____
_____
_____
_____

"ACTION
is the foundational key
to all success."

— *Pablo Picasso*

"I have nothing to offer
BUT BLOOD, TOIL, TEARS AND SWEAT."

— Winston Churchill

Date:

Goals

- [ ]
- [ ]
- [ ]
- [ ]
- [ ]

Total Practice Time:

_____

Date:

Goals

- [ ]
- [ ]
- [ ]
- [ ]
- [ ]

Total Practice Time:

_____

Notes: _____

_____
_____
_____
_____
_____
_____
_____
_____

Notes: _____

_____
_____
_____
_____
_____
_____
_____
_____

Rest Day

Lesson Notes:

_____
_____
_____
_____
_____
_____
_____
_____
_____
_____
_____
_____
_____
_____
_____
_____
_____
_____
_____
_____
_____
_____
_____

Repertoire I Worked On This Week:

_____
_____
_____
_____
_____

Week In Review

What Went Well:

_____
_____
_____
_____
_____
_____
_____

What I Can Do Better:

_____
_____
_____
_____
_____
_____
_____

Don't forget to share your progress with your friends!

#PurposeIn Practice

Objectives
Make Effective

Come to every practice session with realistic goals in mind.

EXPERIMENT TO FIND THAT PERFECT BALANCE OF CHALLENGING
YOURSELF ENOUGH WITHOUT BITING OFF MORE THAN YOU CAN CHEW!

Your Week
At A Glance

MONDAY	TUESDAY	WEDNESDAY

THURSDAY	**Goals** for the week	FRIDAY
	☐ _____ ☐ _____ ☐ _____ ☐ _____ ☐ _____ ☐ _____ ☐ _____ ☐ _____ ☐ _____ ☐ _____ ☐ _____ ☐ _____ ☐ _____ ☐ _____ ☐ _____	

SATURDAY		SUNDAY

"I THINK GOALS SHOULD NEVER BE EASY,
they should force you to work,
even if they are uncomfortable at the time."

— *Michael Phelps*

Date:

Goals

- ☐ _____
- ☐ _____
- ☐ _____
- ☐ _____
- ☐ _____

Total Practice Time:

_____

Date:

Goals

- ☐ _____
- ☐ _____
- ☐ _____
- ☐ _____
- ☐ _____

Total Practice Time:

_____

Notes: _____
_____
_____
_____
_____
_____
_____
_____

Notes: _____
_____
_____
_____
_____
_____
_____
_____

Date:

Goals

☐ _____
☐ _____
☐ _____
☐ _____
☐ _____

Total Practice Time:

_____

Notes: _____
_____
_____
_____
_____
_____
_____
_____

Date:

Goals

☐ _____
☐ _____
☐ _____
☐ _____
☐ _____

Total Practice Time:

_____

Notes: _____
_____
_____
_____
_____
_____
_____
_____

"The greatest danger for most of us
is not that our aim is too high and we miss it,
BUT THAT IT IS TOO LOW AND WE REACH IT."

— Michelangelo

> "THE GREATEST ADVENTURE IS WHAT LIES AHEAD.
> Today and tomorrow are yet to be said.
> The chances, the changes are all yours to make.
> The mold of your life is in your hands to break."
>
> — *J.R.R. Tolkien*

Date:

Goals

- ☐
- ☐
- ☐
- ☐
- ☐

Total Practice Time:

_____

Notes: _____
_____
_____
_____
_____
_____
_____
_____

Date:

Goals

- ☐
- ☐
- ☐
- ☐
- ☐

Total Practice Time:

_____

Notes: _____
_____
_____
_____
_____
_____
_____
_____

Rest Day

Lesson Notes:

_____
_____
_____
_____
_____
_____
_____
_____
_____
_____
_____
_____
_____
_____
_____
_____
_____
_____
_____
_____
_____
_____

Repertoire I Worked On This Week:

_____
_____
_____
_____
_____

Week In Review

What Went Well:

_____
_____
_____
_____
_____

What I Can Do Better:

_____
_____
_____
_____
_____
_____
_____

Don't forget to share your progress with your friends!

#PurposeIn Practice

Practice
As Little As Necessary

Value quality over quantity in your practice sessions. Practice Efficiently!

(RICHARD WEISS' SECRET TO EFFICIENT PRACTICING
AMIDST BUSY TIMES.)

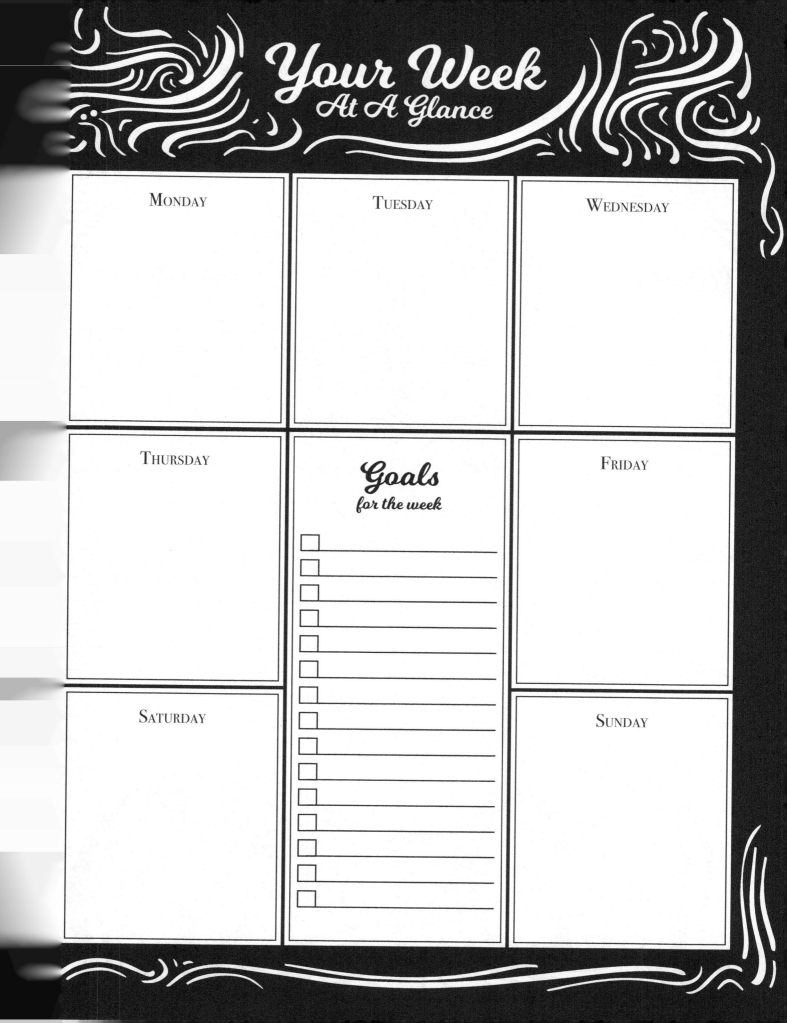

Your Week
At A Glance

MONDAY

TUESDAY

WEDNESDAY

THURSDAY

Goals
for the week

FRIDAY

SATURDAY

SUNDAY

"The successful warrior is the average man, with laser-like focus."

— Bruce Lee

Date:

Goals

- [ ]
- [ ]
- [ ]
- [ ]
- [ ]

Total Practice Time:

Date:

Goals

- [ ]
- [ ]
- [ ]
- [ ]
- [ ]

Total Practice Time:

Notes:

Notes:

Date: _____

Goals

☐ _____
☐ _____
☐ _____
☐ _____
☐ _____

Total Practice Time:

_____

Notes: _____
_____
_____
_____
_____
_____
_____
_____
_____

Date: _____

Goals

☐ _____
☐ _____
☐ _____
☐ _____
☐ _____

Total Practice Time:

_____

Notes: _____
_____
_____
_____
_____
_____
_____
_____
_____

"The difference between a successful person **and others is not a lack of strength,** NOT A LACK OF KNOWLEDGE, BUT RATHER A LACK OF WILL."

— *Vince Lombardi*

"You only have to do a very few things right in your life so long as you don't do too many things wrong."

— Warren Buffett

Date:

Goals

☐ _____
☐ _____
☐ _____
☐ _____
☐ _____

Total Practice Time:

_____

Date:

Goals

☐ _____
☐ _____
☐ _____
☐ _____
☐ _____

Total Practice Time:

_____

<u>Notes:</u> _____
_____
_____
_____
_____
_____
_____
_____

<u>Notes:</u> _____
_____
_____
_____
_____
_____
_____
_____

Rest Day

Lesson Notes:

_____
_____
_____
_____
_____
_____
_____
_____
_____
_____
_____
_____
_____
_____
_____
_____
_____
_____
_____
_____
_____
_____
_____
_____
_____

Repertoire I Worked On This Week:

_____
_____
_____
_____
_____

Week In Review

What Went Well:

_____
_____
_____
_____
_____
_____

What I Can Do Better:

_____
_____
_____
_____
_____
_____
_____

Don't forget to share your progress with your friends!

#PurposeIn Practice

Commit to Six Days Per Week
(But Then Take A Day Off)

Commit to six days of focused,
ambitious, consistent practice.

THEN, DEDICATED ONE DAY TO PURPOSEFUL REST
SO YOU CAN RECHARGE AND GET BACK IN THE GAME.

Your Week
At A Glance

MONDAY

TUESDAY

WEDNESDAY

THURSDAY

Goals
for the week

- [ ]
- [ ]
- [ ]
- [ ]
- [ ]
- [ ]
- [ ]
- [ ]
- [ ]
- [ ]
- [ ]
- [ ]
- [ ]
- [ ]
- [ ]
- [ ]

FRIDAY

SATURDAY

SUNDAY

"Each morning sees some task begun,
Each evening sees it close;
Something attempted, something done,
HAS EARNED A NIGHT'S REPOSE."

— *Henry Wadsworth Longfellow*

Date: _____

Goals

☐ _____
☐ _____
☐ _____
☐ _____
☐ _____

Total Practice Time:

_____

Date: _____

Goals

☐ _____
☐ _____
☐ _____
☐ _____
☐ _____

Total Practice Time:

_____

Notes: _____
_____
_____
_____
_____
_____
_____
_____

Notes: _____
_____
_____
_____
_____
_____
_____
_____

Date:

Goals

☐ _____
☐ _____
☐ _____
☐ _____
☐ _____

Total Practice Time:

_____

Notes: _____
_____
_____
_____
_____
_____
_____
_____
_____

Date:

Goals

☐ _____
☐ _____
☐ _____
☐ _____
☐ _____

Total Practice Time:

_____

Notes: _____
_____
_____
_____
_____
_____
_____
_____
_____

"The old idea of a composer suddenly having a terrific idea
and sitting up all night to write it is nonsense.
NIGHTTIME IS FOR SLEEPING."

— *Benjamin Britten*

"Determine that the thing can and shall be done,
AND THEN WE SHALL FIND THE WAY."

— *Abraham Lincoln*

Date:

Goals

☐ _____
☐ _____
☐ _____
☐ _____
☐ _____

Total Practice Time:

_____

Date:

Goals

☐ _____
☐ _____
☐ _____
☐ _____
☐ _____

Total Practice Time:

_____

Notes: _____
_____
_____
_____
_____
_____
_____
_____

Notes: _____
_____
_____
_____
_____
_____
_____
_____

Rest Day

Lesson Notes:

_____
_____
_____
_____
_____
_____
_____
_____
_____
_____
_____
_____
_____
_____
_____
_____
_____
_____
_____
_____
_____
_____

Repertoire I Worked On This Week:

_____
_____
_____
_____
_____

Week In Review

What Went Well:

_____
_____
_____
_____
_____
_____
_____
_____

What I Can Do Better:

_____
_____
_____
_____
_____
_____
_____

Don't forget to share your progress with your friends!

#PurposeIn Practice

Create A Practice Haven

With a few subtle changes, you can make a haven of your practice room.

TAKE A FEW MOMENTS TO MAKE A PRACTICE SPACE THAT IS CLEAN, INVITING, READY FOR FOCUS, AND ENTIRELY YOURS.

Your Week
At A Glance

MONDAY

TUESDAY

WEDNESDAY

THURSDAY

Goals
for the week

- [ ]
- [ ]
- [ ]
- [ ]
- [ ]
- [ ]
- [ ]
- [ ]
- [ ]
- [ ]
- [ ]
- [ ]
- [ ]

FRIDAY

SATURDAY

SUNDAY

"*We shape our dwellings,*
and afterwards our dwellings shape us."

— *Winston Churchill*

Date:

Goals

- [ ]
- [ ]
- [ ]
- [ ]
- [ ]

Total Practice Time:

_____

Date:

Goals

- [ ]
- [ ]
- [ ]
- [ ]
- [ ]

Total Practice Time:

_____

Notes: _____

_____
_____
_____
_____
_____
_____

Notes: _____

_____
_____
_____
_____
_____
_____

Date: **Goals**

☐ _____
☐ _____
☐ _____
☐ _____
☐ _____

Total Practice Time:

_____

Notes:

_____
_____
_____
_____
_____
_____
_____
_____

Date: **Goals**

☐ _____
☐ _____
☐ _____
☐ _____
☐ _____

Total Practice Time:

_____

Notes:

_____
_____
_____
_____
_____
_____
_____
_____

"SIMPLICITY
is the ultimate
Sophistication."

— _Leonardo Da Vinci_

"Three rules of work: Out of clutter find simplicity;
From discord find harmony;
IN THE MIDDLE OF DIFFICULTY LIES OPPORTUNITY."

— *Albert Einstein*

Date:

Goals

☐ _____
☐ _____
☐ _____
☐ _____
☐ _____

Total Practice Time:

_____

Notes: _____
_____
_____
_____
_____
_____
_____

Date:

Goals

☐ _____
☐ _____
☐ _____
☐ _____
☐ _____

Total Practice Time:

_____

Notes: _____
_____
_____
_____
_____
_____
_____

Rest Day

Lesson Notes:

_____
_____
_____
_____
_____
_____
_____
_____
_____
_____
_____
_____
_____
_____
_____
_____
_____
_____
_____
_____
_____
_____

Repertoire I Worked On This Week:

_____
_____
_____
_____
_____

Week In Review

What Went Well:

_____
_____
_____
_____
_____
_____
_____

What I Can Do Better:

_____
_____
_____
_____
_____
_____
_____

Don't forget to share your progress with your friends!

#PurposeIn Practice

Put Your Phone On Airplane Mode

Cultivate true focus in your practice room with this simple trick.

IF EVERY PRACTICER PLACED THEIR PHONE IN AIRPLANE MODE DURING THEIR PRACTICE SESSIONS, IT'S HARD TO SAY HOW MANY VIRTUOSOS THE WORLD WOULD PRODUCE!

Your Week
At A Glance

MONDAY

TUESDAY

WEDNESDAY

THURSDAY

Goals
for the week

- [ ]
- [ ]
- [ ]
- [ ]
- [ ]
- [ ]
- [ ]
- [ ]
- [ ]
- [ ]
- [ ]
- [ ]
- [ ]
- [ ]
- [ ]

FRIDAY

SATURDAY

SUNDAY

"I was obliged to be industrious.
Whoever is equally industrious will succeed equally well."

— J.S. Bach

Date:

Goals

- [ ]
- [ ]
- [ ]
- [ ]
- [ ]

Total Practice Time:

Date:

Goals

- [ ]
- [ ]
- [ ]
- [ ]
- [ ]

Total Practice Time:

Notes:

Notes:

Date: _____

Goals

- ☐ _____
- ☐ _____
- ☐ _____
- ☐ _____
- ☐ _____

Total Practice Time:

_____

Notes: _____

_____
_____
_____
_____
_____
_____
_____
_____
_____

Date: _____

Goals

- ☐ _____
- ☐ _____
- ☐ _____
- ☐ _____
- ☐ _____

Total Practice Time:

_____

Notes: _____

_____
_____
_____
_____
_____
_____
_____
_____
_____

"The three great essentials
to achieve anything worthwhile are:
Hard work, stick-to-itiveness, and common sense."

— *Thomas Edison*

"Concentrate all your thoughts upon the work at hand.
The sun's rays do not burn
UNTIL BROUGHT TO A FOCUS."

— *Alexander Graham Bell*

Date:

Goals

☐ _____
☐ _____
☐ _____
☐ _____
☐ _____

Total Practice Time:
_____

Date:

Goals

☐ _____
☐ _____
☐ _____
☐ _____
☐ _____

Total Practice Time:
_____

Notes: _____
_____
_____
_____
_____
_____
_____
_____

Notes: _____
_____
_____
_____
_____
_____
_____
_____

Rest Day

Lesson Notes:

_____
_____
_____
_____
_____
_____
_____
_____
_____
_____
_____
_____
_____
_____
_____
_____
_____
_____
_____
_____
_____
_____
_____

Repertoire I Worked On This Week:

_____
_____
_____
_____

Week In Review

What Went Well:

_____
_____
_____
_____
_____
_____

What I Can Do Better:

_____
_____
_____
_____
_____
_____

Don't forget to share your progress with your friends!

#PurposeIn Practice

Those Who Band Together
Stand Together

It takes a village to raise a musician.

BAND TOGETHER WITH A COMMUNITY WHO WILL BE WILLING TO HELP
YOU AS YOU WORK TOWARDS GETTING BETTER AT YOUR INSTRUMENT.

Your Week
At A Glance

MONDAY

TUESDAY

WEDNESDAY

THURSDAY

Goals
for the week

- [ ] _____
- [ ] _____
- [ ] _____
- [ ] _____
- [ ] _____
- [ ] _____
- [ ] _____
- [ ] _____
- [ ] _____
- [ ] _____
- [ ] _____
- [ ] _____
- [ ] _____
- [ ] _____

FRIDAY

SATURDAY

SUNDAY

"MUSIC IS THE SOCIAL ACT
of communication among people,
a gesture of friendship, the strongest there is."

— Malcolm Arnold

Date:

Goals

Total Practice Time:

Notes:

Date:

Goals

Total Practice Time:

Notes:

Date: _____

Goals

☐ _____
☐ _____
☐ _____
☐ _____
☐ _____

Total Practice Time:

_____

Notes: _____
_____
_____
_____
_____
_____
_____
_____
_____

Date: _____

Goals

☐ _____
☐ _____
☐ _____
☐ _____
☐ _____

Total Practice Time:

_____

Notes: _____
_____
_____
_____
_____
_____
_____
_____
_____

"I alone cannot change the world,
but I can cast a stone across the waters to create many ripples."

— *Mother Teresa*

*"**Alone, we can do so little;**
together, we can do so much."*

— Helen Keller

Date:

Goals

- ☐ _____
- ☐ _____
- ☐ _____
- ☐ _____
- ☐ _____

Total Practice Time:

_____

Date:

Goals

- ☐ _____
- ☐ _____
- ☐ _____
- ☐ _____
- ☐ _____

Total Practice Time:

_____

Notes:
_____
_____
_____
_____
_____
_____
_____
_____

Notes:
_____
_____
_____
_____
_____
_____
_____
_____

Rest Day

Lesson Notes:

_____
_____
_____
_____
_____
_____
_____
_____
_____
_____
_____
_____
_____
_____
_____
_____
_____
_____
_____
_____
_____
_____

Repertoire I Worked On This Week:

_____
_____
_____
_____

Week In Review

What Went Well:

_____
_____
_____
_____
_____
_____

What I Can Do Better:

_____
_____
_____
_____
_____
_____

Don't forget to share your progress with your friends!

#PurposeIn Practice

You Are An Athlete

Athletes take their goals so seriously that every moment matters.

CREATE A DAILY ROUTINE THAT PRIORITIZES THE CARE OF YOUR BODY
AS YOU WORK TOWARDS MEETING YOUR BIGGEST PRACTICE GOALS.

Your Week
At A Glance

MONDAY

TUESDAY

WEDNESDAY

THURSDAY

Goals
for the week

- [ ]
- [ ]
- [ ]
- [ ]
- [ ]
- [ ]
- [ ]
- [ ]
- [ ]
- [ ]
- [ ]
- [ ]
- [ ]
- [ ]
- [ ]

FRIDAY

SATURDAY

SUNDAY

"THE ONLY DIFFERENCE
between success and failure
is the ability to take action."

— *Alexander Graham Bell*

Date:

Goals

☐ _____
☐ _____
☐ _____
☐ _____
☐ _____

Total Practice Time:
_____

Date:

Goals

☐ _____
☐ _____
☐ _____
☐ _____
☐ _____

Total Practice Time:
_____

Notes: _____
_____
_____
_____
_____
_____
_____
_____

Notes: _____
_____
_____
_____
_____
_____
_____
_____

3xp

3xp

Date: _____

Goals

☐ _____
☐ _____
☐ _____
☐ _____
☐ _____

Total Practice Time:

_____

Notes: _____
_____
_____
_____
_____
_____
_____
_____
_____

Date: _____

Goals

☐ _____
☐ _____
☐ _____
☐ _____
☐ _____

Total Practice Time:

_____

Notes: _____
_____
_____
_____
_____
_____
_____
_____
_____

"I've failed over and over again in my life.
And that is why I succeed."

— *Michael Jordan*

"*If you fail to prepare,*
YOU'RE PREPARED TO FAIL."

— *Mark Spitz*

Date: _____

Goals

☐ _____
☐ _____
☐ _____
☐ _____
☐ _____

Total Practice Time:
_____

Date: _____

Goals

☐ _____
☐ _____
☐ _____
☐ _____
☐ _____

Total Practice Time:
_____

Notes: _____
_____
_____
_____
_____
_____
_____
_____
_____

Notes: _____
_____
_____
_____
_____
_____
_____
_____
_____

Rest Day

Lesson Notes:

_____
_____
_____
_____
_____
_____
_____
_____
_____
_____
_____
_____
_____
_____
_____
_____
_____
_____
_____

Repertoire I Worked On This Week:

_____
_____
_____
_____

Week In Review

What Went Well:

_____
_____
_____
_____
_____
_____

What I Can Do Better:

_____
_____
_____
_____
_____
_____
_____

Don't forget to share your progress with your friends!

#PurposeIn Practice

Mindfulness Is Key

Being present is one of the most important secrets to great practice.

GIVE YOUR FULLEST ATTENTION TO EVERY MOMENT OF YOUR PRACTICE
SESSION, AND WATCH YOUR PRODUCTIVITY BLOSSOM.

Your Week
At A Glance

MONDAY

TUESDAY

WEDNESDAY

THURSDAY

Goals
for the week

- [ ] _____
- [ ] _____
- [ ] _____
- [ ] _____
- [ ] _____
- [ ] _____
- [ ] _____
- [ ] _____
- [ ] _____
- [ ] _____
- [ ] _____
- [ ] _____
- [ ] _____
- [ ] _____
- [ ] _____

FRIDAY

SATURDAY

SUNDAY

"Obstacles are those frightful things you see when you take your eyes off your goal."

— Henry Ford

Date:

Goals

- [ ]
- [ ]
- [ ]
- [ ]
- [ ]

Total Practice Time:
_____

Date:

Goals

- [ ]
- [ ]
- [ ]
- [ ]
- [ ]

Total Practice Time:
_____

Notes: _____

_____
_____
_____
_____
_____
_____

Notes: _____

_____
_____
_____
_____
_____
_____

Date: _____

Goals

- [ ]
- [ ]
- [ ]
- [ ]
- [ ]

Total Practice Time:

_____

Notes: _____

_____
_____
_____
_____
_____
_____
_____
_____

Date: _____

Goals

- [ ]
- [ ]
- [ ]
- [ ]
- [ ]

Total Practice Time:

_____

Notes: _____

_____
_____
_____
_____
_____
_____
_____
_____

"Only through focus
can you do world class things,
NO MATTER HOW CAPABLE YOU ARE. "

— *Bill Gates*

"QUALITY
is not an act,
it is a habit."

— Aristotle

Date:

Goals

- ☐
- ☐
- ☐
- ☐
- ☐

Total Practice Time:

Date:

Goals

- ☐
- ☐
- ☐
- ☐
- ☐

Total Practice Time:

Notes:

Notes:

Rest Day

Lesson Notes:

_____
_____
_____
_____
_____
_____
_____
_____
_____
_____
_____
_____
_____
_____
_____
_____
_____
_____
_____
_____
_____
_____

Repertoire I Worked On This Week:

_____
_____
_____
_____

Week In Review

What Went Well:

_____
_____
_____
_____
_____
_____
_____

What I Can Do Better:

_____
_____
_____
_____
_____
_____
_____

Don't forget to share your progress with your friends!

#PurposeIn Practice

You Are Your Own Worst Critic

Of all the people in the world, you are the biggest expert on yourself.

EXPECTING MORE OF YOURSELF WILL GROW YOU IN UNIMAGINABLE WAYS.

Your Week
At A Glance

MONDAY

TUESDAY

WEDNESDAY

THURSDAY

Goals
for the week

- [ ]
- [ ]
- [ ]
- [ ]
- [ ]
- [ ]
- [ ]
- [ ]
- [ ]
- [ ]
- [ ]
- [ ]
- [ ]
- [ ]

FRIDAY

SATURDAY

SUNDAY

"I am hitting my head against the walls,
BUT THE WALLS ARE GIVING WAY."

— *Gustav Mahler*

Date:

Goals

☐ _____
☐ _____
☐ _____
☐ _____
☐ _____

Total Practice Time:

_____

Date:

Goals

☐ _____
☐ _____
☐ _____
☐ _____
☐ _____

Total Practice Time:

_____

Notes: _____
_____
_____
_____
_____
_____
_____
_____

Notes: _____
_____
_____
_____
_____
_____
_____
_____

Date: _____

Goals

☐ _____
☐ _____
☐ _____
☐ _____
☐ _____

Total Practice Time:
_____

Notes: _____
_____
_____
_____
_____
_____
_____
_____
_____

Date: _____

Goals

☐ _____
☐ _____
☐ _____
☐ _____
☐ _____

Total Practice Time:
_____

Notes: _____
_____
_____
_____
_____
_____
_____
_____
_____

"IT IS ONLY THROUGH FAILURE *and through experiment* that we learn and grow."

— Isaac Stern

"Don't let the noise of others' opinions drown out your own inner voice."

— Steve Jobs

Date:

Goals

☐
☐
☐
☐
☐

Total Practice Time:
_____

Date:

Goals

☐
☐
☐
☐
☐

Total Practice Time:
_____

Notes: _____
_____
_____
_____
_____
_____
_____

Notes: _____
_____
_____
_____
_____
_____
_____

Rest Day

Lesson Notes:

_____
_____
_____
_____
_____
_____
_____
_____
_____
_____
_____
_____
_____
_____
_____
_____
_____
_____
_____
_____
_____

Repertoire I Worked On This Week:

_____
_____
_____
_____

Week In Review

What Went Well:

_____
_____
_____
_____
_____

What I Can Do Better:

_____
_____
_____
_____
_____
_____
_____

Don't forget to share your progress with your friends!

#PurposeIn Practice

Can't
Is A Bad Word

Destroy negative self talk
before it destroys you.

RESPECT YOURSELF MORE BY NEVER TELLING YOURSELF YOU CAN'T DO
SOMETHING. INSTEAD, GET IN THERE AND DO IT!

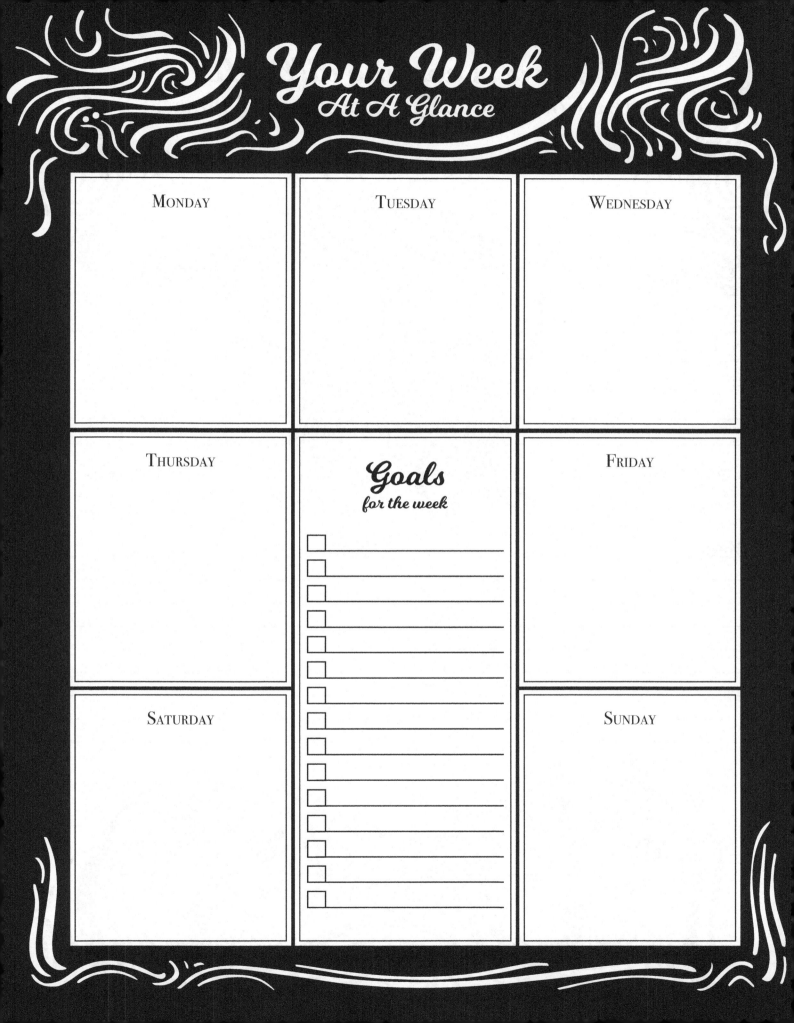

Your Week
At A Glance

MONDAY	TUESDAY	WEDNESDAY

THURSDAY	Goals *for the week*	FRIDAY
	☐ _____	
	☐ _____	
	☐ _____	
	☐ _____	
	☐ _____	
	☐ _____	

SATURDAY		SUNDAY
	☐ _____	
	☐ _____	
	☐ _____	
	☐ _____	
	☐ _____	
	☐ _____	
	☐ _____	

"There is nothing difficult,
there are only new things, unaccustomed things."

— Carlos Salzedo

Date: _____

Goals

- ☐
- ☐
- ☐
- ☐
- ☐

Total Practice Time: _____

Date: _____

Goals

- ☐
- ☐
- ☐
- ☐
- ☐

Total Practice Time: _____

Notes: _____

_____
_____
_____
_____
_____
_____

Notes: _____

_____
_____
_____
_____
_____
_____

Date: _____

Goals

- [ ] _____
- [ ] _____
- [ ] _____
- [ ] _____
- [ ] _____

Total Practice Time:
_____

Notes: _____
_____
_____
_____
_____
_____
_____
_____
_____

Date: _____

Goals

- [ ] _____
- [ ] _____
- [ ] _____
- [ ] _____
- [ ] _____

Total Practice Time:
_____

Notes: _____
_____
_____
_____
_____
_____
_____
_____
_____

"There's nothing remarkable about it.
All one has to do is hit the right keys at the right time
AND THE INSTRUMENT PLAYS ITSELF."

— J.S. Bach

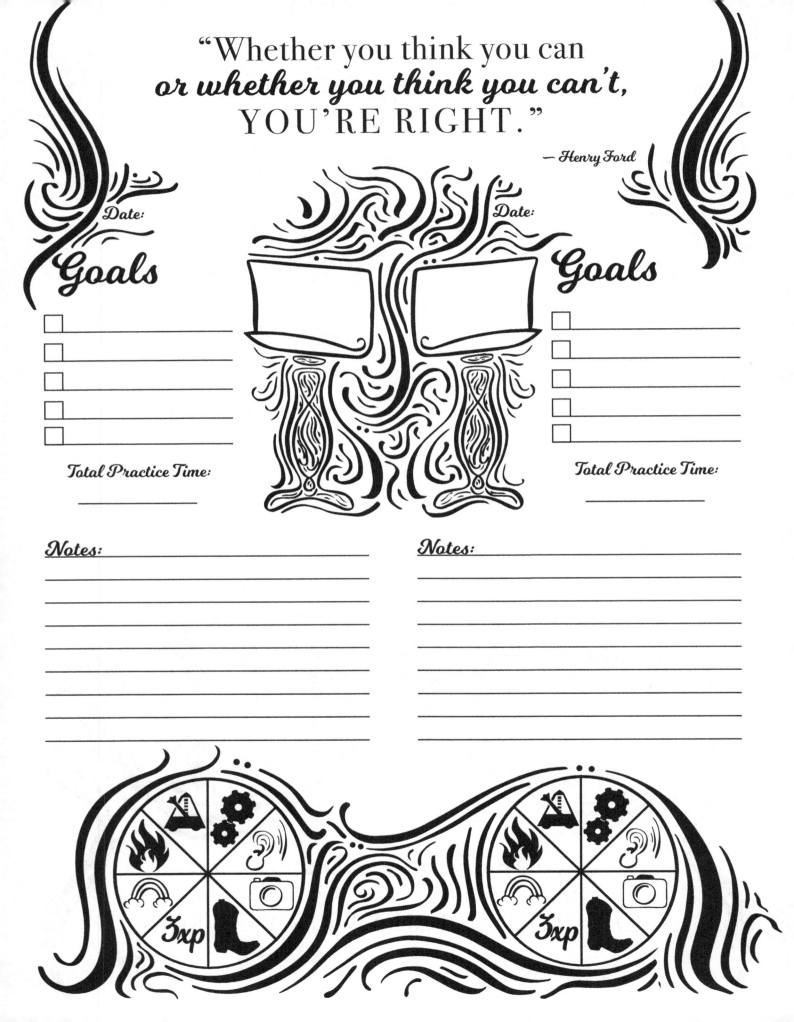

"Whether you think you can
or whether you think you can't,
YOU'RE RIGHT."

— Henry Ford

Date:

Goals

☐
☐
☐
☐
☐

Total Practice Time:

_____

Notes:

Date:

Goals

☐
☐
☐
☐
☐

Total Practice Time:

_____

Notes:

Rest Day

Lesson Notes:

_____
_____
_____
_____
_____
_____
_____
_____
_____
_____
_____
_____
_____
_____
_____
_____
_____
_____
_____
_____
_____
_____
_____
_____

Repertoire I Worked On This Week:

_____
_____
_____
_____
_____

Week In Review

What Went Well:

_____
_____
_____
_____
_____

What I Can Do Better:

_____
_____
_____
_____
_____
_____
_____

Don't forget to share your progress with your friends!

#PurposeIn Practice

Sign Up For Boot Camp

Slow, single-volume practice is Yolanda Kondonassis' key to quick learning.

AS COUNTERINTUITIVE AS IT SOUNDS, PRACTICING EVERYTHING AS SLOWLY AS POSSIBLE IS THE FASTEST WAY TO LEARN YOUR NOTES.

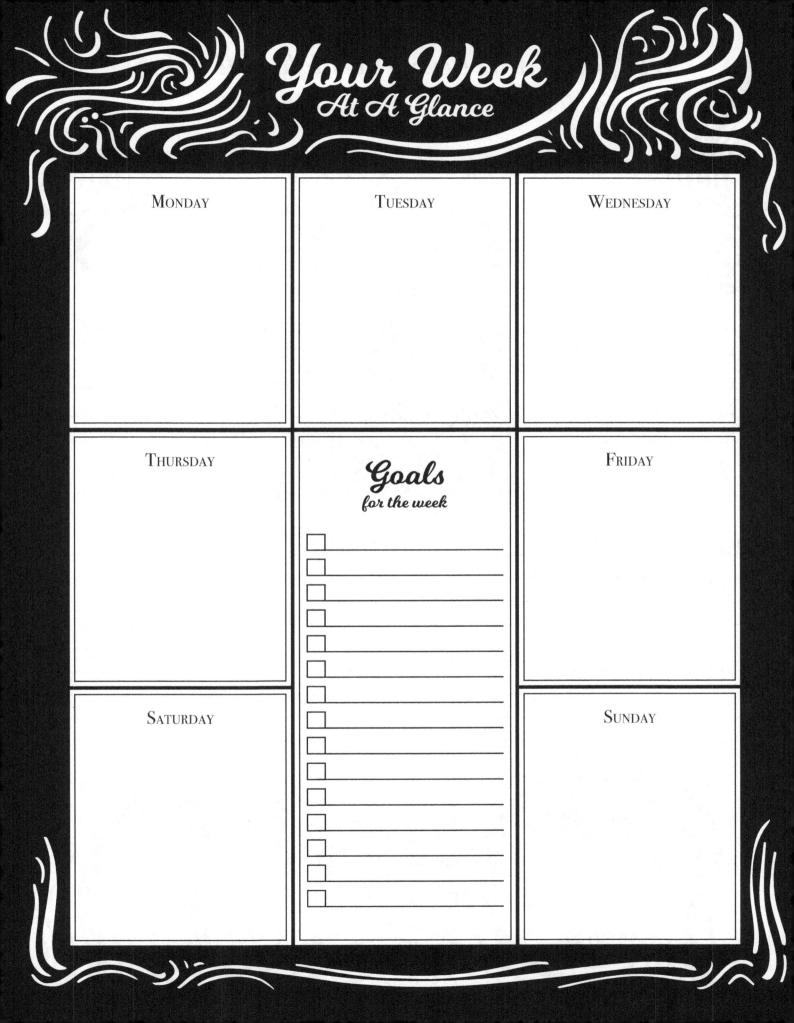

Your Week
At A Glance

MONDAY

TUESDAY

WEDNESDAY

THURSDAY

Goals
for the week

- [ ] _____
- [ ] _____
- [ ] _____
- [ ] _____
- [ ] _____
- [ ] _____
- [ ] _____
- [ ] _____
- [ ] _____
- [ ] _____
- [ ] _____
- [ ] _____
- [ ] _____
- [ ] _____

FRIDAY

SATURDAY

SUNDAY

"All I can do is devote the night to the task,
for it cannot be managed otherwise."

— W.A. Mozart

Date:

Goals

- ☐ _____
- ☐ _____
- ☐ _____
- ☐ _____
- ☐ _____

Total Practice Time:

_____

Date:

Goals

- ☐ _____
- ☐ _____
- ☐ _____
- ☐ _____
- ☐ _____

Total Practice Time:

_____

Notes: _____
_____
_____
_____
_____
_____

Notes: _____
_____
_____
_____
_____
_____

Date: _____

Goals

- [ ] _____
- [ ] _____
- [ ] _____
- [ ] _____
- [ ] _____

Total Practice Time:

_____

Notes: _____

_____
_____
_____
_____
_____
_____
_____
_____

Date: _____

Goals

- [ ] _____
- [ ] _____
- [ ] _____
- [ ] _____
- [ ] _____

Total Practice Time:

_____

Notes: _____

_____
_____
_____
_____
_____
_____
_____
_____

"One must always practice slowly.
If you learn something slowly,
you forget it slowly."

— *Itzhak Perlman*

"Time is the best of critics;
and patience the best of teachers."

— Frederic Chopin

Date:

Goals

☐ _____
☐ _____
☐ _____
☐ _____
☐ _____

Total Practice Time:

_____

Date:

Goals

☐ _____
☐ _____
☐ _____
☐ _____
☐ _____

Total Practice Time:

_____

Notes: _____
_____
_____
_____
_____
_____
_____

Notes: _____
_____
_____
_____
_____
_____
_____

Rest Day

Lesson Notes:

_____
_____
_____
_____
_____
_____
_____
_____
_____
_____
_____
_____
_____
_____
_____
_____
_____
_____
_____

Repertoire I Worked On This Week:

_____
_____
_____
_____

Week In Review

What Went Well:

_____
_____
_____
_____
_____
_____

What I Can Do Better:

_____
_____
_____
_____
_____
_____
_____

Don't forget to share your progress with your friends!

#PurposeIn Practice

Your Metronome
Is Your Best Friend

Look up to your metronome as your most valued practice companion.

BECOMING BEST FRIENDS WITH YOUR METRONOME WILL PUSH YOU TOWARD HIGHER LEVELS OF PERFECTION.

Your Week
At A Glance

MONDAY

TUESDAY

WEDNESDAY

THURSDAY

Goals
for the week

- [ ]
- [ ]
- [ ]
- [ ]
- [ ]
- [ ]
- [ ]
- [ ]
- [ ]
- [ ]
- [ ]
- [ ]
- [ ]
- [ ]
- [ ]

FRIDAY

SATURDAY

SUNDAY

"**The best way to learn**
IS THROUGH THE POWERFUL FORCE OF RHYTHM."

— *W.A. Mozart*

Date:

Goals

☐ _____
☐ _____
☐ _____
☐ _____
☐ _____

Total Practice Time:
_____

Date:

Goals

☐ _____
☐ _____
☐ _____
☐ _____
☐ _____

Total Practice Time:
_____

Notes: _____
_____
_____
_____
_____
_____
_____
_____

Notes: _____
_____
_____
_____
_____
_____
_____
_____

Date:

Goals

☐ _____
☐ _____
☐ _____
☐ _____
☐ _____

Total Practice Time:
_____

Notes: _____
_____
_____
_____
_____
_____
_____
_____

Date:

Goals

☐ _____
☐ _____
☐ _____
☐ _____
☐ _____

Total Practice Time:
_____

Notes: _____
_____
_____
_____
_____
_____
_____
_____

"Rhythm is something you either have
or don't have, but when you have it,
YOU HAVE IT ALL OVER."

— Elvis Presley

"Music and rhythm find their way *into the secret places of the soul.*"

— *Plato*

Date:

Goals

- [ ]
- [ ]
- [ ]
- [ ]
- [ ]

Total Practice Time:

Date:

Goals

- [ ]
- [ ]
- [ ]
- [ ]
- [ ]

Total Practice Time:

Notes:

Notes:

Rest Day

Lesson Notes:

_____
_____
_____
_____
_____
_____
_____
_____
_____
_____
_____
_____
_____
_____
_____
_____
_____
_____
_____
_____
_____
_____
_____
_____

Repertoire I Worked On This Week:

_____
_____
_____
_____
_____

Week In Review

What Went Well:

_____
_____
_____
_____
_____
_____

What I Can Do Better:

_____
_____
_____
_____
_____
_____

Don't forget to share your progress with your friends!

#PurposeIn Practice

Be A Stable-Mucker

Being a musician requires constant maintenance and labor. But it's worth it.

THE FEWER OXEN A FARMER HAS, THE LEAST AMOUNT OF MAINTENANCE HIS STABLE REQUIRES. BUT THE MORE OXEN A FARMER HAS, THE MORE HARVEST HE CAN BRING IN.

Your Week
At A Glance

MONDAY

TUESDAY

WEDNESDAY

THURSDAY

Goals
for the week

- [ ]
- [ ]
- [ ]
- [ ]
- [ ]
- [ ]
- [ ]
- [ ]
- [ ]
- [ ]
- [ ]
- [ ]
- [ ]
- [ ]

FRIDAY

SATURDAY

SUNDAY

"WITHOUT STOPPING, WITHOUT HASTE,
carefully taking a step at a time forward
will surely get you there."

— Schiniki Suzuki

Date:

Goals

- [ ] _____
- [ ] _____
- [ ] _____
- [ ] _____
- [ ] _____

Total Practice Time:
_____

Date:

Goals

- [ ] _____
- [ ] _____
- [ ] _____
- [ ] _____
- [ ] _____

Total Practice Time:
_____

Notes: _____
_____
_____
_____
_____
_____
_____
_____

Notes: _____
_____
_____
_____
_____
_____
_____
_____

Date:

Goals

☐ _____
☐ _____
☐ _____
☐ _____
☐ _____

Total Practice Time:
_____

Notes: _____
_____
_____
_____
_____
_____
_____
_____
_____

Date:

Goals

☐ _____
☐ _____
☐ _____
☐ _____
☐ _____

Total Practice Time:
_____

Notes: _____
_____
_____
_____
_____
_____
_____
_____
_____

"Slow and Steady
Wins the Race."

— Aesop

"*If you really look closely,*
MOST OVERNIGHT SUCCESSES TOOK A LONG TIME."

— Steve Jobs

Date:

Goals

- [ ]
- [ ]
- [ ]
- [ ]
- [ ]

Total Practice Time:

_____

Date:

Goals

- [ ]
- [ ]
- [ ]
- [ ]
- [ ]

Total Practice Time:

_____

Notes: _____
_____
_____
_____
_____
_____
_____

Notes: _____
_____
_____
_____
_____
_____
_____

"*If you really look closely,*

Rest Day

Lesson Notes:

_____
_____
_____
_____
_____
_____
_____
_____
_____
_____
_____
_____
_____
_____
_____
_____
_____
_____
_____
_____
_____
_____

Repertoire I Worked On This Week:

_____
_____
_____
_____
_____

Week In Review

What Went Well:

_____
_____
_____
_____
_____
_____

What I Can Do Better:

_____
_____
_____
_____
_____
_____

Don't forget to share your progress with your friends!

#PurposeIn Practice

Don't Be A Trained Bird

C.P.E. Bach's best advice
for playing from the soul.

MOVE BEYOND THE NOTES ON THE PAGE AND READ BETWEEN THE LINES.
YOU HAVE A LOT TO SAY WITH YOUR MUSIC: HOW WILL YOU SAY IT?

Your Week
At A Glance

MONDAY

TUESDAY

WEDNESDAY

THURSDAY

Goals
for the week

- [ ]
- [ ]
- [ ]
- [ ]
- [ ]
- [ ]
- [ ]
- [ ]
- [ ]
- [ ]
- [ ]
- [ ]
- [ ]
- [ ]
- [ ]

FRIDAY

SATURDAY

SUNDAY

"Play from the soul,
not like a trained bird!"

— C.P.E. Bach

Date:

Goals

- ☐ _____
- ☐ _____
- ☐ _____
- ☐ _____
- ☐ _____

Total Practice Time:
_____

Notes: _____
_____
_____
_____
_____
_____
_____

Date:

Goals

- ☐ _____
- ☐ _____
- ☐ _____
- ☐ _____
- ☐ _____

Total Practice Time:
_____

Notes: _____
_____
_____
_____
_____
_____
_____

Date:

Goals

☐ _____
☐ _____
☐ _____
☐ _____
☐ _____

Total Practice Time:
_____

Notes: _____
_____
_____
_____
_____
_____
_____
_____

Date:

Goals

☐ _____
☐ _____
☐ _____
☐ _____
☐ _____

Total Practice Time:
_____

Notes: _____
_____
_____
_____
_____
_____
_____
_____

3xp

3xp

"Persevere, do not only practice your art,
but endeavor also to fathom its inner meaning;
IT DESERVES THIS EFFORT."

— Ludwig van Beethoven

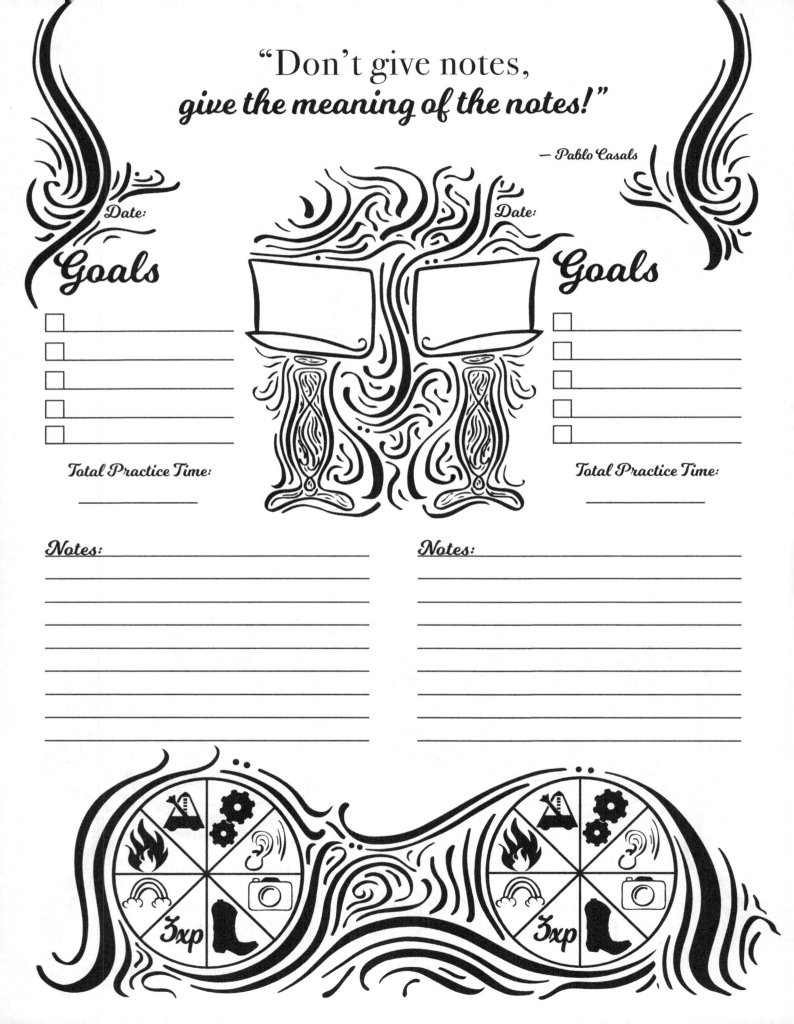

> "Don't give notes,
> give the meaning of the notes!"
>
> — Pablo Casals

Date: _____

Goals

- ☐ _____
- ☐ _____
- ☐ _____
- ☐ _____
- ☐ _____

Total Practice Time:

_____

Date: _____

Goals

- ☐ _____
- ☐ _____
- ☐ _____
- ☐ _____
- ☐ _____

Total Practice Time:

_____

Notes: _____

_____

_____

_____

_____

_____

_____

_____

Notes: _____

_____

_____

_____

_____

_____

_____

_____

Rest Day

Lesson Notes:

_____
_____
_____
_____
_____
_____
_____
_____
_____
_____
_____
_____
_____
_____
_____
_____
_____
_____
_____
_____
_____
_____
_____
_____

Repertoire I Worked On This Week:

_____
_____
_____
_____

Week In Review

What Went Well:

_____
_____
_____
_____
_____

What I Can Do Better:

_____
_____
_____
_____
_____
_____

Don't forget to share your progress with your friends!

#PurposeIn Practice

Record Yourself

Give yourself the eye-opening perspective of the listener

TAKE YOUR PLAYING TO THE NEXT LEVEL BY RECORDING YOUR PRACTICE SESSIONS AND LISTENING WITH A CRITICAL EAR.

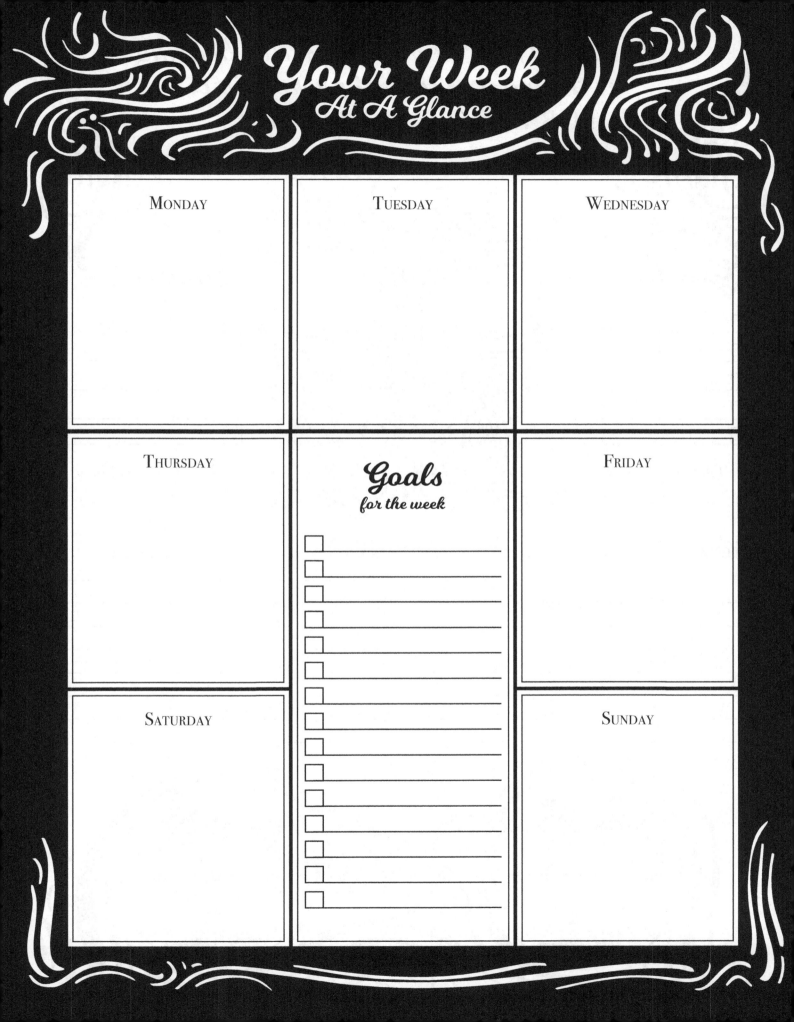

Your Week
At A Glance

MONDAY

TUESDAY

WEDNESDAY

THURSDAY

Goals
for the week

- [ ]
- [ ]
- [ ]
- [ ]
- [ ]
- [ ]
- [ ]
- [ ]
- [ ]
- [ ]
- [ ]
- [ ]
- [ ]
- [ ]
- [ ]

FRIDAY

SATURDAY

SUNDAY

"The ability for honest, objective hearing
is the most essential prerequisite
FOR EFFICIENT PRACTICE."

— *Ivan Galamian*

Date: _____

Goals

☐ _____
☐ _____
☐ _____
☐ _____
☐ _____

Total Practice Time:
_____

Date: _____

Goals

☐ _____
☐ _____
☐ _____
☐ _____
☐ _____

Total Practice Time:
_____

Notes: _____
_____
_____
_____
_____
_____
_____

Notes: _____
_____
_____
_____
_____
_____
_____

Date: _____

Goals

- ☐ _____
- ☐ _____
- ☐ _____
- ☐ _____
- ☐ _____

Total Practice Time:

_____

Notes: _____

_____
_____
_____
_____
_____
_____
_____
_____

Date: _____

Goals

- ☐ _____
- ☐ _____
- ☐ _____
- ☐ _____
- ☐ _____

Total Practice Time:

_____

Notes: _____

_____
_____
_____
_____
_____
_____
_____
_____

3xp

3xp

"The most important thing to do *is really listen.*"

— *Itzhak Perlman*

"I listened more than I studied,
therefore little by little my knowledge
AND ABILITY WERE DEVELOPED."

— *Joseph Haydn*

Date:

Goals

- ☐ _____
- ☐ _____
- ☐ _____
- ☐ _____
- ☐ _____

Total Practice Time:

_____

Date:

Goals

- ☐ _____
- ☐ _____
- ☐ _____
- ☐ _____
- ☐ _____

Total Practice Time:

_____

Notes: _____

_____
_____
_____
_____
_____
_____
_____

Notes: _____

_____
_____
_____
_____
_____
_____
_____

Rest Day

Lesson Notes:

_____
_____
_____
_____
_____
_____
_____
_____
_____
_____
_____
_____
_____
_____
_____
_____
_____
_____
_____
_____
_____
_____

Repertoire I Worked On This Week:

_____
_____
_____
_____

Week In Review

What Went Well:

_____
_____
_____
_____
_____
_____
_____

What I Can Do Better:

_____
_____
_____
_____
_____
_____
_____

Don't forget to share your progress with your friends!

#PurposeIn Practice

Become A Student of the Greatest Artists

You can invite the greatest artists into your practice room.

TAKE ADVANTAGE OF THE VAST TREASURE TROVE OF GREAT
RECORDINGS YOU HAVE AT YOUR FINGERTIPS.

Your Week
At A Glance

MONDAY

TUESDAY

WEDNESDAY

THURSDAY

Goals
for the week

- [ ]
- [ ]
- [ ]
- [ ]
- [ ]
- [ ]
- [ ]
- [ ]
- [ ]
- [ ]
- [ ]
- [ ]
- [ ]
- [ ]

FRIDAY

SATURDAY

SUNDAY

> *"Lesser artists borrow,*
> *great artists steal."*
>
> — *Igor Stravinsky*

Date: _____

Goals

- ☐ _____
- ☐ _____
- ☐ _____
- ☐ _____
- ☐ _____

Total Practice Time:

_____

Date: _____

Goals

- ☐ _____
- ☐ _____
- ☐ _____
- ☐ _____
- ☐ _____

Total Practice Time:

_____

Notes: _____

_____

_____

_____

_____

_____

_____

Notes: _____

_____

_____

_____

_____

_____

_____

Date: _____

Goals

- [ ] _____
- [ ] _____
- [ ] _____
- [ ] _____
- [ ] _____

Total Practice Time:

_____

Date: _____

Goals

- [ ] _____
- [ ] _____
- [ ] _____
- [ ] _____
- [ ] _____

Total Practice Time:

_____

<u>Notes:</u> _____

_____

_____

_____

_____

_____

_____

_____

<u>Notes:</u> _____

_____

_____

_____

_____

_____

_____

_____

"There is not a famous master
whose music I have not industriously studied
THROUGH MANY TIMES."

— W.A. Mozart

"Learn all there is to learn, and then choose your own path."

— G.F. Handel

Date:

Goals

- [ ]
- [ ]
- [ ]
- [ ]
- [ ]

Total Practice Time:
_____

Notes: _____
_____
_____
_____
_____
_____
_____

Date:

Goals

- [ ]
- [ ]
- [ ]
- [ ]
- [ ]

Total Practice Time:
_____

Notes: _____
_____
_____
_____
_____
_____
_____

Rest Day

Lesson Notes:

_____
_____
_____
_____
_____
_____
_____
_____
_____
_____
_____
_____
_____
_____
_____
_____
_____
_____
_____
_____
_____

Repertoire I Worked On This Week:

_____
_____
_____
_____

Week In Review

What Went Well:

_____
_____
_____
_____
_____

What I Can Do Better:

_____
_____
_____
_____
_____

Don't forget to share your progress with your friends!

#PurposeIn Practice

Memorize Methodically

Though valuable, muscle memory is risky to rely on entirely.

DEVELOP METHODICAL MEMORIZATION STRATEGIES
SO THAT YOU DON'T CHOKE ON PERFORMANCE DAY.

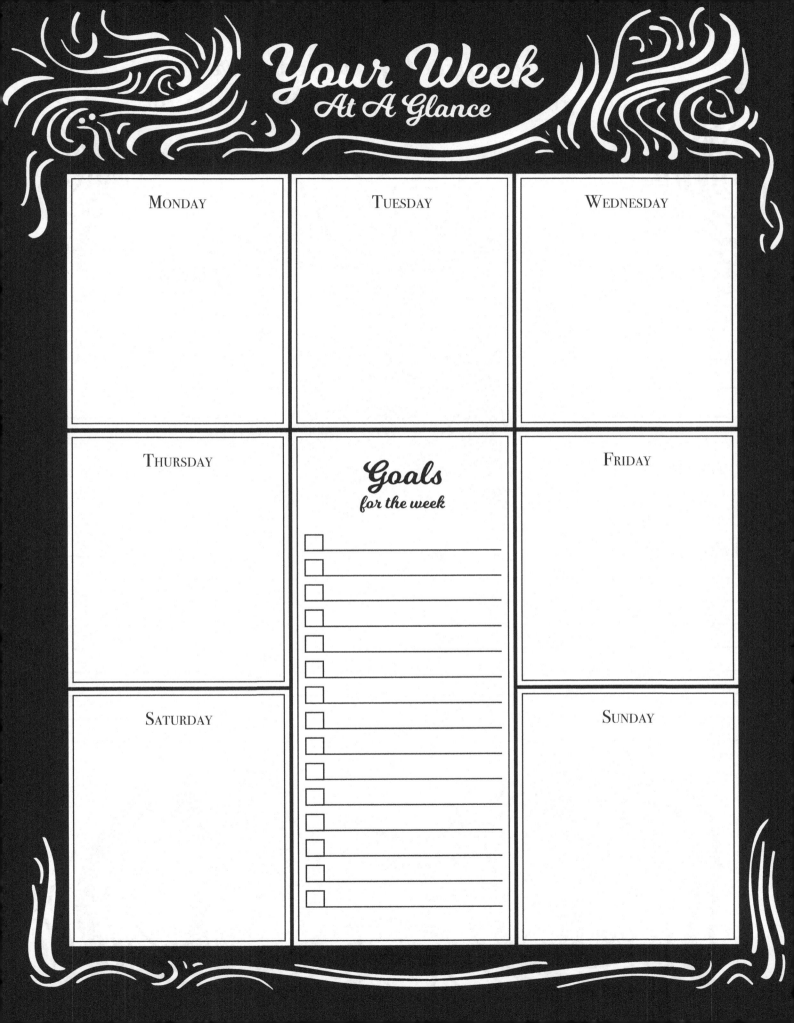

Your Week
At A Glance

MONDAY

TUESDAY

WEDNESDAY

THURSDAY

Goals
for the week

FRIDAY

SATURDAY

SUNDAY

"*Every difficulty slurred over will be a ghost to disturb your repose later on.*"

— Frederic Chopin

Date:

Goals

☐ _____
☐ _____
☐ _____
☐ _____
☐ _____

Total Practice Time:

_____

Date:

Goals

☐ _____
☐ _____
☐ _____
☐ _____
☐ _____

Total Practice Time:

_____

Notes: _____
_____
_____
_____
_____
_____
_____

Notes: _____
_____
_____
_____
_____
_____
_____

3xp

3xp

Date: _____

Goals

☐ _____
☐ _____
☐ _____
☐ _____
☐ _____

Total Practice Time:

_____

Notes: _____
_____
_____
_____
_____
_____
_____
_____
_____

Date: _____

Goals

☐ _____
☐ _____
☐ _____
☐ _____
☐ _____

Total Practice Time:

_____

Notes: _____
_____
_____
_____
_____
_____
_____
_____
_____

"Do one thing every day
THAT SCARES YOU."

— Eleanor Roosevelt

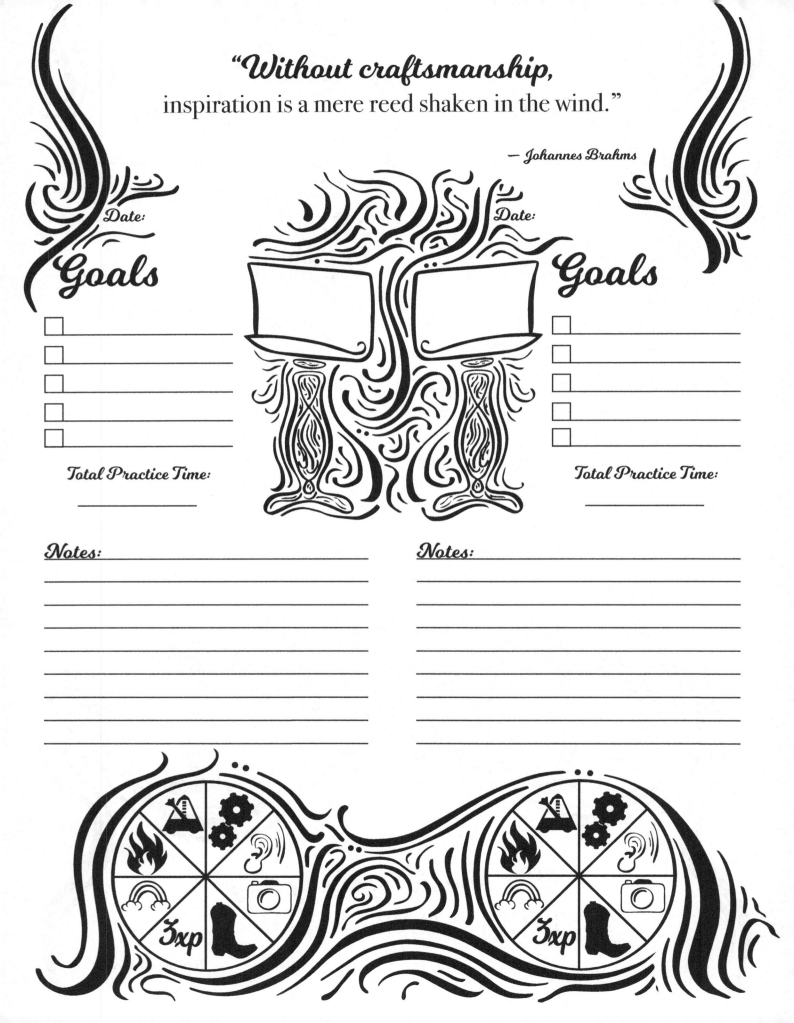

"Without craftsmanship,
inspiration is a mere reed shaken in the wind."

— Johannes Brahms

Date:

Goals

- [ ]
- [ ]
- [ ]
- [ ]
- [ ]

Total Practice Time:

_____

Date:

Goals

- [ ]
- [ ]
- [ ]
- [ ]
- [ ]

Total Practice Time:

_____

Notes: _____

_____

_____

_____

_____

_____

_____

Notes: _____

_____

_____

_____

_____

_____

_____

Rest Day

Lesson Notes:

_____
_____
_____
_____
_____
_____
_____
_____
_____
_____
_____
_____
_____
_____
_____
_____
_____
_____
_____
_____
_____
_____
_____
_____

Repertoire I Worked On This Week:

_____
_____
_____
_____

Week In Review

What Went Well:

_____
_____
_____
_____
_____

What I Can Do Better:

_____
_____
_____
_____
_____

Don't forget to share your progress with your friends!

#PurposeIn Practice

Polish
Toward Perfection

Take your performance repertoire to the next level.

As you near a performance, polish your repertoire in a way that pushes you towards a higher version of perfection.

Your Week
At A Glance

MONDAY

TUESDAY

WEDNESDAY

THURSDAY

Goals
for the week

- [ ] _____
- [ ] _____
- [ ] _____
- [ ] _____
- [ ] _____
- [ ] _____
- [ ] _____
- [ ] _____
- [ ] _____
- [ ] _____
- [ ] _____
- [ ] _____
- [ ] _____
- [ ] _____
- [ ] _____

FRIDAY

SATURDAY

SUNDAY

"**Energy and persistence**
CONQUER ALL THINGS."

— *Benjamin Franklin*

Date:

Goals

☐ _____
☐ _____
☐ _____
☐ _____
☐ _____

Total Practice Time:
_____

Date:

Goals

☐ _____
☐ _____
☐ _____
☐ _____
☐ _____

Total Practice Time:
_____

Notes: _____
_____
_____
_____
_____
_____
_____

Notes: _____
_____
_____
_____
_____
_____
_____

Date:

Goals

☐ _____
☐ _____
☐ _____
☐ _____
☐ _____

Total Practice Time:

_____

Notes: _____
_____
_____
_____
_____
_____
_____
_____
_____

Date:

Goals

☐ _____
☐ _____
☐ _____
☐ _____
☐ _____

Total Practice Time:

_____

Notes: _____
_____
_____
_____
_____
_____
_____
_____
_____

"Inspiration is a guest

that does not willingly visit the lazy."

— Pyotr Ilyich Tchaikovsky

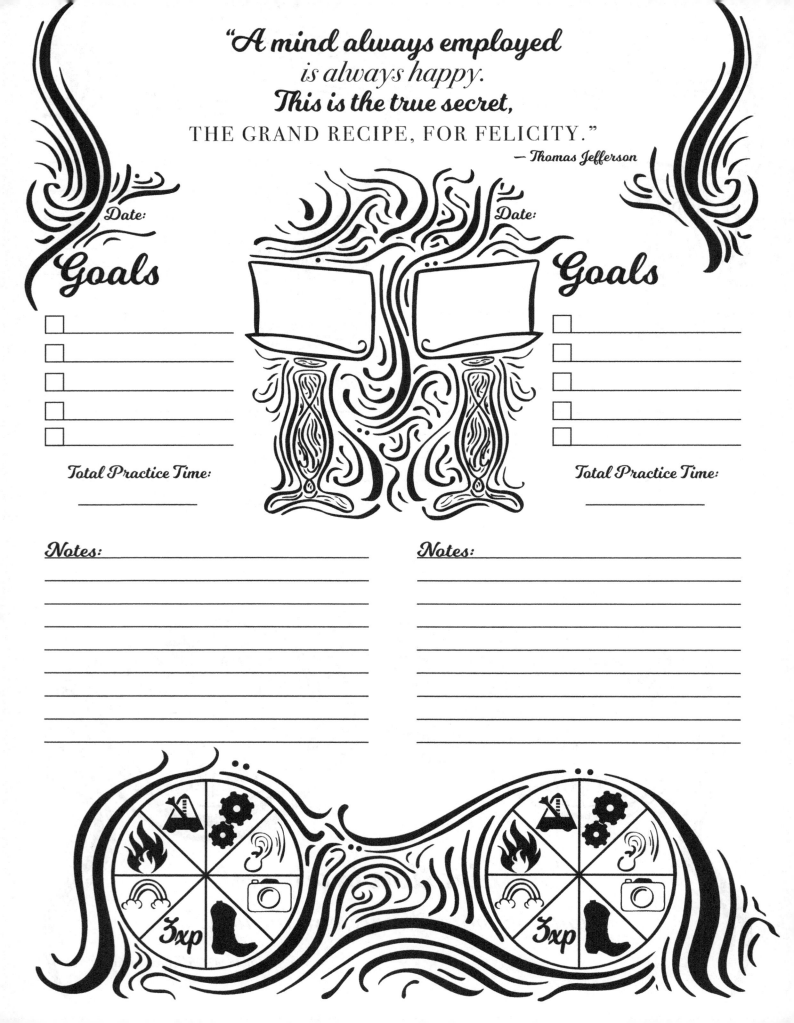

"*A mind always employed*
is always happy.
This is the true secret,
THE GRAND RECIPE, FOR FELICITY."
— *Thomas Jefferson*

Date:

Goals

- [ ]
- [ ]
- [ ]
- [ ]
- [ ]

Total Practice Time:

_____

Date:

Goals

- [ ]
- [ ]
- [ ]
- [ ]
- [ ]

Total Practice Time:

_____

Notes: _____

_____
_____
_____
_____
_____
_____

Notes: _____

_____
_____
_____
_____
_____
_____

Rest Day

Lesson Notes:

_____
_____
_____
_____
_____
_____
_____
_____
_____
_____
_____
_____
_____
_____
_____
_____
_____
_____
_____
_____
_____
_____

Week In Review

What Went Well:

_____
_____
_____
_____
_____
_____

What I Can Do Better:

_____
_____
_____
_____
_____
_____
_____

Don't forget to share your progress with your friends!

#PurposeIn Practice

Repertoire I Worked On This Week:

_____
_____
_____
_____
_____

Deadlines
Make the World Go Round

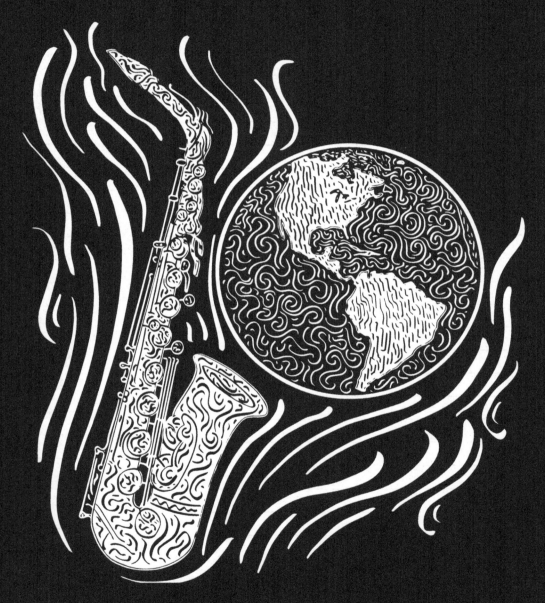

Setting a deadline is like a magical key that unlocks the vast treasure trove of motivation.

A DEADLINE IS A SUREFIRE WAY TO GIVE YOURSELF ENOUGH MOTIVATION TO ACCOMPLISH YOUR GOALS.

Your Week
At A Glance

MONDAY

TUESDAY

WEDNESDAY

THURSDAY

Goals
for the week

- [ ] _____
- [ ] _____
- [ ] _____
- [ ] _____
- [ ] _____
- [ ] _____
- [ ] _____
- [ ] _____
- [ ] _____
- [ ] _____
- [ ] _____
- [ ] _____
- [ ] _____
- [ ] _____
- [ ] _____

FRIDAY

SATURDAY

SUNDAY

"The way to get started is to quit talking
and begin doing."

— *Walt Disney*

Date:

Goals

☐ _____
☐ _____
☐ _____
☐ _____
☐ _____

Total Practice Time:
_____

Date:

Goals

☐ _____
☐ _____
☐ _____
☐ _____
☐ _____

Total Practice Time:
_____

Notes: _____
_____
_____
_____
_____
_____
_____
_____

Notes: _____
_____
_____
_____
_____
_____
_____
_____

Date:

Goals

☐ _____
☐ _____
☐ _____
☐ _____
☐ _____

Total Practice Time:

_____

Notes: _____
_____
_____
_____
_____
_____
_____
_____

Date:

Goals

☐ _____
☐ _____
☐ _____
☐ _____
☐ _____

Total Practice Time:

_____

Notes: _____
_____
_____
_____
_____
_____
_____
_____

3xp

3xp

"The secret to getting ahead is getting started."

— *Mark Twain*

"To achieve great things, two things are needed;
a plan, and not quite enough time."

— *Leonard Bernstein*

Date:

Goals

☐ _____
☐ _____
☐ _____
☐ _____
☐ _____

Total Practice Time:
_____

Date:

Goals

☐ _____
☐ _____
☐ _____
☐ _____
☐ _____

Total Practice Time:
_____

Notes: _____
_____
_____
_____
_____
_____
_____

Notes: _____
_____
_____
_____
_____
_____
_____

Rest Day

Lesson Notes:

_____
_____
_____
_____
_____
_____
_____
_____
_____
_____
_____
_____
_____
_____
_____
_____
_____
_____
_____
_____
_____
_____
_____
_____

Week In Review

What Went Well:

_____
_____
_____
_____
_____
_____

What I Can Do Better:

_____
_____
_____
_____
_____
_____

Don't forget to share your progress with your friends!

#PurposeIn Practice

Repertoire I Worked On This Week:

_____
_____
_____
_____

You Are The Instrument

Don't fight your instrument to get your ideas across.

USE YOURSELF AS THE INSTRUMENT TO COMMUNICATE SOMETHING BIGGER THAN YOURSELF.

Your Week
At A Glance

MONDAY

TUESDAY

WEDNESDAY

THURSDAY

Goals
for the week

- [ ]
- [ ]
- [ ]
- [ ]
- [ ]
- [ ]
- [ ]
- [ ]
- [ ]
- [ ]
- [ ]
- [ ]
- [ ]
- [ ]
- [ ]

FRIDAY

SATURDAY

SUNDAY

"To send light into the darkness of men's hearts, **such is the duty of the artist.**"

— Robert Schumann

Date:

Goals

- [ ]
- [ ]
- [ ]
- [ ]
- [ ]

Total Practice Time:

Notes:

Date:

Goals

- [ ]
- [ ]
- [ ]
- [ ]
- [ ]

Total Practice Time:

Notes:

Date:

Goals

☐ _____
☐ _____
☐ _____
☐ _____
☐ _____

Total Practice Time:

_____

Notes: _____

_____
_____
_____
_____
_____
_____
_____
_____
_____

Date:

Goals

☐ _____
☐ _____
☐ _____
☐ _____
☐ _____

Total Practice Time:

_____

Notes: _____

_____
_____
_____
_____
_____
_____
_____
_____
_____

"I should be sorry if I only entertained them.
I WISH TO MAKE THEM BETTER."

— G.F. Handel

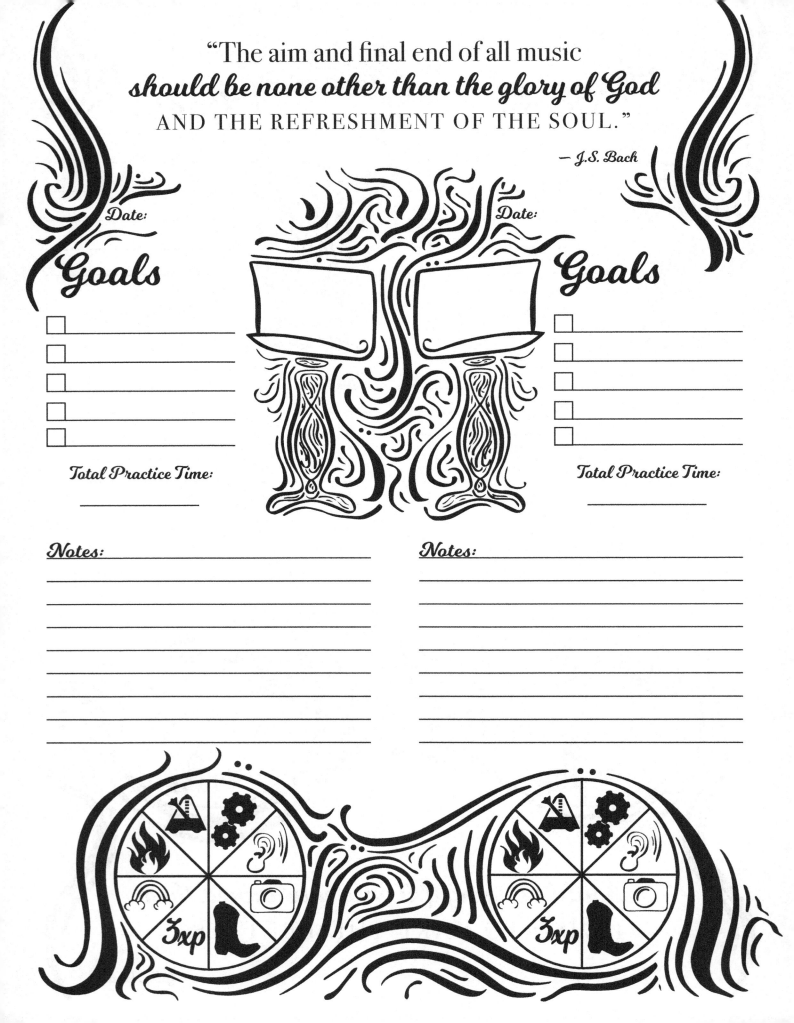

"The aim and final end of all music
should be none other than the glory of God
AND THE REFRESHMENT OF THE SOUL."

— J.S. Bach

Date:

Goals

- [ ]
- [ ]
- [ ]
- [ ]
- [ ]

Total Practice Time:

_____

Date:

Goals

- [ ]
- [ ]
- [ ]
- [ ]
- [ ]

Total Practice Time:

_____

Notes: _____

_____

_____

_____

_____

_____

_____

Notes: _____

_____

_____

_____

_____

_____

_____

Rest Day

Lesson Notes:

_____
_____
_____
_____
_____
_____
_____
_____
_____
_____
_____
_____
_____
_____
_____
_____
_____
_____
_____
_____
_____
_____
_____
_____
_____

Week In Review

What Went Well:

_____
_____
_____
_____
_____

What I Can Do Better:

_____
_____
_____
_____
_____
_____
_____

Don't forget to share your progress with your friends!

#PurposeIn Practice

Repertoire I Worked On This Week:

_____
_____
_____
_____
_____

To Be Exemplary
Learn By Example

Give yourself the gift of looking up to a
few worthy role models.

LET YOURSELF LEARN AND STUDY THE METHODS OF A FEW GREAT
ARTISTS, AND THEIR EXAMPLE COULD IN TURN MAKE YOU EXEMPLARY.

Your Week
At A Glance

MONDAY

TUESDAY

WEDNESDAY

THURSDAY

Goals
for the week

- [ ]
- [ ]
- [ ]
- [ ]
- [ ]
- [ ]
- [ ]
- [ ]
- [ ]
- [ ]
- [ ]
- [ ]
- [ ]
- [ ]
- [ ]
- [ ]

FRIDAY

SATURDAY

SUNDAY

"An artist's sphere of influence is the world."

— Carl Maria von Weber

Date: _____

Goals

- ☐ _____
- ☐ _____
- ☐ _____
- ☐ _____
- ☐ _____

Total Practice Time:

_____

Date: _____

Goals

- ☐ _____
- ☐ _____
- ☐ _____
- ☐ _____
- ☐ _____

Total Practice Time:

_____

Notes: _____
_____
_____
_____
_____
_____
_____

Notes: _____
_____
_____
_____
_____
_____
_____

Date: _____

Goals

☐ _____
☐ _____
☐ _____
☐ _____
☐ _____

Total Practice Time:
_____

Notes: _____
_____
_____
_____
_____
_____
_____
_____

Date: _____

Goals

☐ _____
☐ _____
☐ _____
☐ _____
☐ _____

Total Practice Time:
_____

Notes: _____
_____
_____
_____
_____
_____
_____
_____

"If I have seen further
it is by standing on the shoulders of giants."

— Isaac Newton

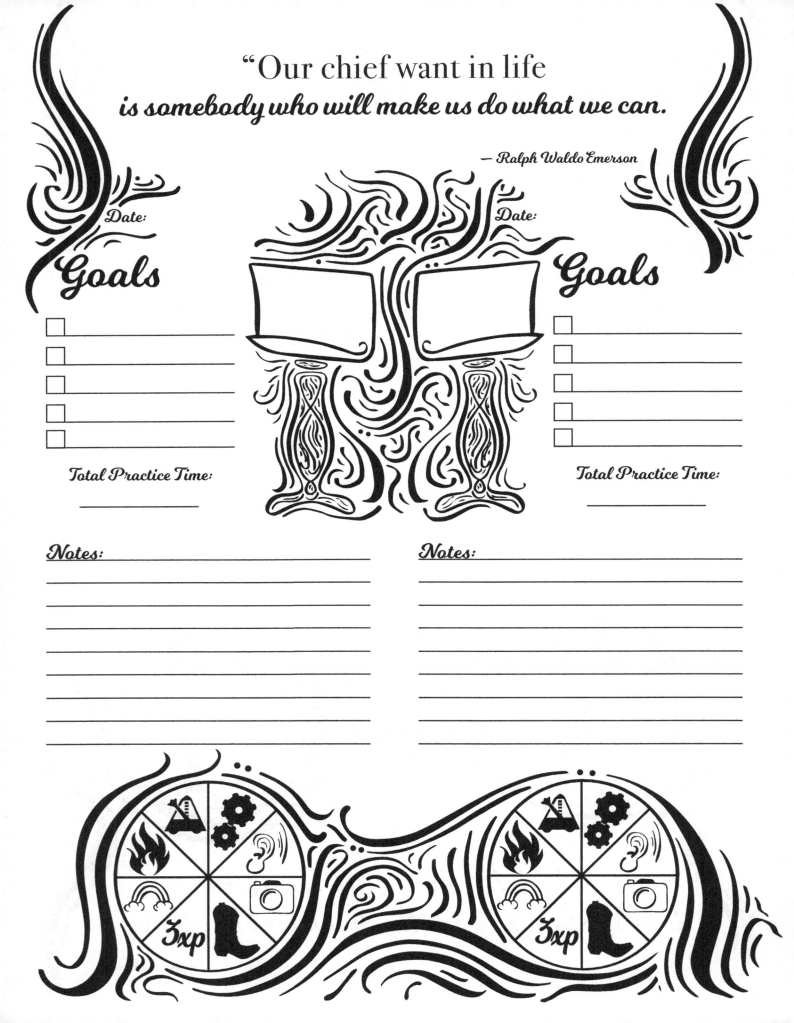

"Our chief want in life
is somebody who will make us do what we can.

— Ralph Waldo Emerson

Date:

Goals

☐ _____
☐ _____
☐ _____
☐ _____
☐ _____

Total Practice Time:
_____

Date:

Goals

☐ _____
☐ _____
☐ _____
☐ _____
☐ _____

Total Practice Time:
_____

Notes: _____
_____
_____
_____
_____
_____
_____

Notes: _____
_____
_____
_____
_____
_____
_____

Rest Day

Lesson Notes:

_____
_____
_____
_____
_____
_____
_____
_____
_____
_____
_____
_____
_____
_____
_____
_____
_____
_____
_____
_____
_____
_____
_____
_____

Repertoire I Worked On This Week:

_____
_____
_____
_____

Week In Review

What Went Well:

_____
_____
_____
_____
_____
_____
_____

What I Can Do Better:

_____
_____
_____
_____
_____
_____
_____

Don't forget to share your progress with your friends!

#PurposeIn Practice

Become A Submarine

Don't let too many of life's worries leak into your practice sessions.

LIKE SECTIONS OF A SUBMARINE, COMPARTMENTALIZE THE DIFFERENT AREAS OF YOUR LIFE SO THAT IF ONE LEAKS, THE DAMAGE IS CONTAINED AND YOU CAN KEEP GOING.

Your Week
At A Glance

MONDAY

TUESDAY

WEDNESDAY

THURSDAY

Goals
for the week

- [ ] _____
- [ ] _____
- [ ] _____
- [ ] _____
- [ ] _____
- [ ] _____
- [ ] _____
- [ ] _____
- [ ] _____
- [ ] _____
- [ ] _____
- [ ] _____
- [ ] _____
- [ ] _____
- [ ] _____
- [ ] _____

FRIDAY

SATURDAY

SUNDAY

> *"Just remember, you're not a machine."*
>
> — Alice Chalifoux

Date: _____

Goals

☐ _____
☐ _____
☐ _____
☐ _____
☐ _____

Total Practice Time:

_____

Date: _____

Goals

☐ _____
☐ _____
☐ _____
☐ _____
☐ _____

Total Practice Time:

_____

Notes: _____

_____
_____
_____
_____
_____
_____

Notes: _____

_____
_____
_____
_____
_____
_____

Date:

Goals

☐ _____
☐ _____
☐ _____
☐ _____
☐ _____

Total Practice Time:
_____

Notes: _____
_____
_____
_____
_____
_____
_____
_____

Date:

Goals

☐ _____
☐ _____
☐ _____
☐ _____
☐ _____

Total Practice Time:
_____

Notes: _____
_____
_____
_____
_____
_____
_____
_____

"THE PESSIMIST SEES DIFFICULTY
in every opportunity.
The optimist sees opportunity in every difficulty."

— *Winston Churchill*

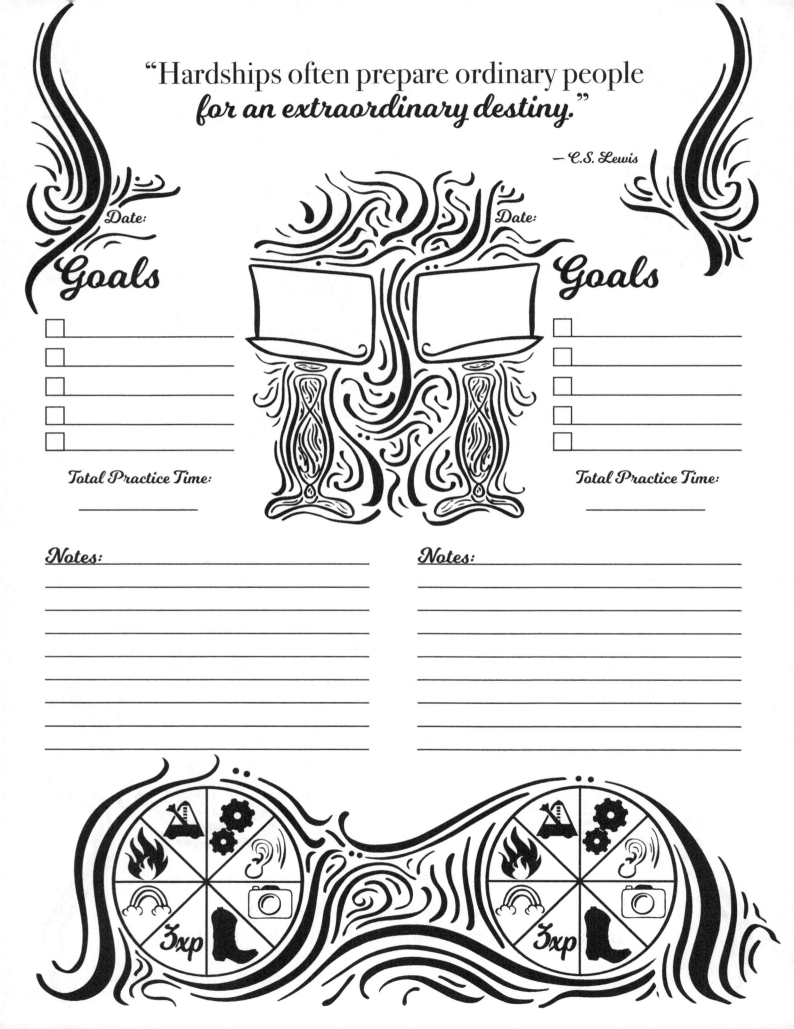

"Hardships often prepare ordinary people
for an extraordinary destiny."

— *C.S. Lewis*

Date:

Goals

☐ _____
☐ _____
☐ _____
☐ _____
☐ _____

Total Practice Time:

_____

Date:

Goals

☐ _____
☐ _____
☐ _____
☐ _____
☐ _____

Total Practice Time:

_____

Notes: _____

_____
_____
_____
_____
_____
_____
_____

Notes: _____

_____
_____
_____
_____
_____
_____
_____

Rest Day

Lesson Notes:

_____
_____
_____
_____
_____
_____
_____
_____
_____
_____
_____
_____
_____
_____
_____
_____
_____
_____
_____
_____
_____
_____
_____
_____
_____
_____

Repertoire I Worked On This Week:

_____
_____
_____
_____
_____

Week In Review

What Went Well:

_____
_____
_____
_____
_____
_____

What I Can Do Better:

_____
_____
_____
_____
_____
_____
_____

Don't forget to share your progress with your friends!

#PurposeIn Practice

You Are Worth More Than
Your Practice Session

You have immense value with or without your instrument in hand.

PUT THINGS INTO PERSPECTIVE AND REALIZE THAT YOUR PRACTICE SESSION, YOUR INSTRUMENT, AND EVEN YOUR CAREER DOESN'T DEFINE WHO YOU ARE.

Your Week
At A Glance

MONDAY

TUESDAY

WEDNESDAY

THURSDAY

Goals
for the week

- ☐
- ☐
- ☐
- ☐
- ☐
- ☐
- ☐
- ☐
- ☐
- ☐
- ☐
- ☐
- ☐
- ☐
- ☐

FRIDAY

SATURDAY

SUNDAY

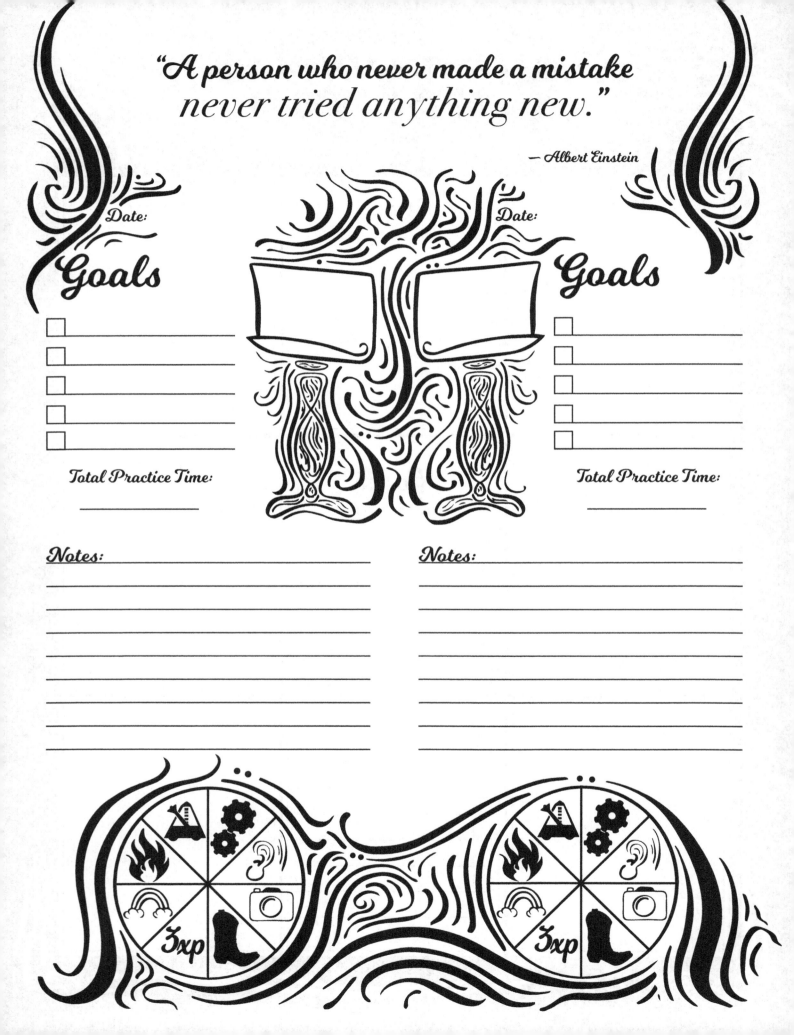

"*A person who never made a mistake
never tried anything new.*"

— Albert Einstein

Date: _____

Goals

☐ _____
☐ _____
☐ _____
☐ _____
☐ _____

Total Practice Time:

_____

Date: _____

Goals

☐ _____
☐ _____
☐ _____
☐ _____
☐ _____

Total Practice Time:

_____

Notes: _____
_____
_____
_____
_____
_____
_____

Notes: _____
_____
_____
_____
_____
_____
_____

Date:

Goals

☐ _____
☐ _____
☐ _____
☐ _____
☐ _____

Total Practice Time:

_____

Notes:
_____
_____
_____
_____
_____
_____
_____
_____

Date:

Goals

☐ _____
☐ _____
☐ _____
☐ _____
☐ _____

Total Practice Time:

_____

Notes:
_____
_____
_____
_____
_____
_____
_____
_____

"May your work be in
keeping with your purpose."

— *Leonardo da Vinci*

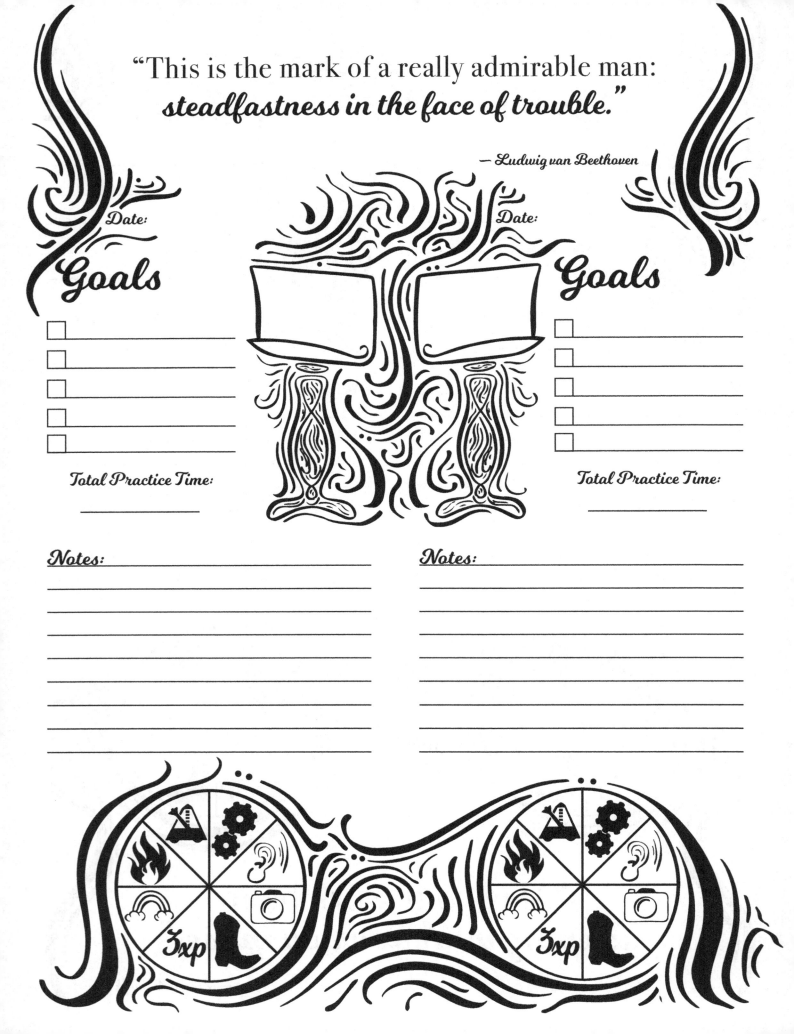

"This is the mark of a really admirable man: *steadfastness in the face of trouble.*"

— Ludwig van Beethoven

Date:

Goals

☐
☐
☐
☐
☐

Total Practice Time:

_____

Date:

Goals

☐
☐
☐
☐
☐

Total Practice Time:

_____

Notes: _____

_____
_____
_____
_____
_____
_____

Notes: _____

_____
_____
_____
_____
_____
_____

Rest Day

Lesson Notes:

_____
_____
_____
_____
_____
_____
_____
_____
_____
_____
_____
_____
_____
_____
_____
_____
_____
_____
_____
_____
_____
_____
_____

Repertoire I Worked On This Week:

_____
_____
_____
_____

Week In Review

What Went Well:

_____
_____
_____
_____
_____

What I Can Do Better:

_____
_____
_____
_____
_____
_____
_____

Don't forget to share your progress with your friends!

#PurposeIn Practice

End On A High Note

No matter how frustrated you are, end with something that is doable and satisfying.

ENDING ON A POSITIVE NOTE WILL MAKE YOU WANT TO COME BACK AND KEEP MEETING YOUR GOALS.

Your Week
At A Glance

MONDAY

TUESDAY

WEDNESDAY

THURSDAY

Goals
for the week

- [ ] _____
- [ ] _____
- [ ] _____
- [ ] _____
- [ ] _____
- [ ] _____
- [ ] _____
- [ ] _____
- [ ] _____
- [ ] _____
- [ ] _____
- [ ] _____
- [ ] _____
- [ ] _____
- [ ] _____
- [ ] _____

FRIDAY

SATURDAY

SUNDAY

"Nothing right can be accomplished in *art without enthusiasm.*"

— Robert Schumann

Date:

Goals

☐ _____
☐ _____
☐ _____
☐ _____
☐ _____

Total Practice Time:

_____

Date:

Goals

☐ _____
☐ _____
☐ _____
☐ _____
☐ _____

Total Practice Time:

_____

Notes: _____
_____
_____
_____
_____
_____
_____

Notes: _____
_____
_____
_____
_____
_____
_____

Date: _____

Goals

- [ ] _____
- [ ] _____
- [ ] _____
- [ ] _____
- [ ] _____

Total Practice Time:

_____

Notes: _____

_____
_____
_____
_____
_____
_____
_____
_____

Date: _____

Goals

- [ ] _____
- [ ] _____
- [ ] _____
- [ ] _____
- [ ] _____

Total Practice Time:

_____

Notes: _____

_____
_____
_____
_____
_____
_____
_____
_____

"Believe you can
AND YOU'RE HALFWAY THERE."

— Theodore Roosevelt

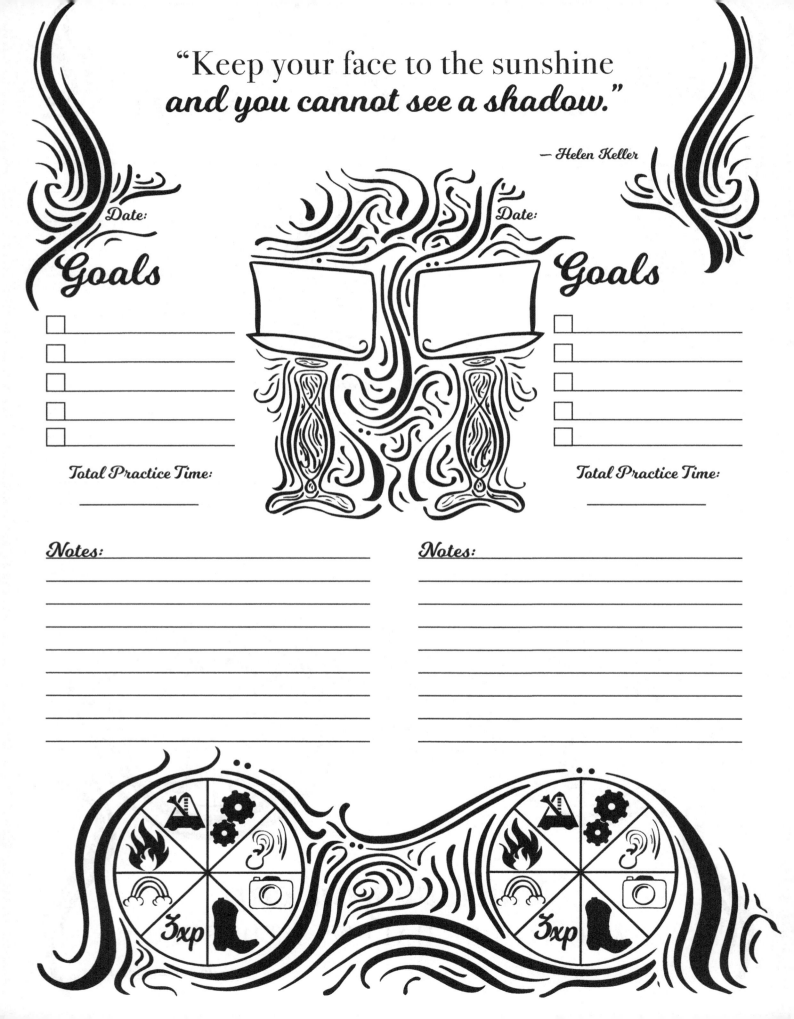

"Keep your face to the sunshine
and you cannot see a shadow."

— *Helen Keller*

Date:

Goals

☐ _____
☐ _____
☐ _____
☐ _____
☐ _____

Total Practice Time:

_____

Date:

Goals

☐ _____
☐ _____
☐ _____
☐ _____
☐ _____

Total Practice Time:

_____

Notes: _____

_____

_____

_____

_____

_____

_____

Notes: _____

_____

_____

_____

_____

_____

_____

Rest Day

Lesson Notes:

_____
_____
_____
_____
_____
_____
_____
_____
_____
_____
_____
_____
_____
_____
_____
_____
_____
_____
_____
_____
_____
_____

Repertoire I Worked On This Week:

_____
_____
_____
_____

Week In Review

What Went Well:

_____
_____
_____
_____
_____
_____

What I Can Do Better:

_____
_____
_____
_____
_____
_____
_____
_____

Don't forget to share your progress with your friends!

#PurposeIn Practice

Don't Forget to Live

Get out of your practice room every now and then to experience life.

THE BEST WAY TO MATURE IN MUSICALITY IS TO DRAW FROM
LIFE-ENRICHING MOMENTS. YOU DON'T FIND THOSE IN A PRACTICE ROOM.

Your Week
At A Glance

MONDAY

TUESDAY

WEDNESDAY

THURSDAY

Goals
for the week

- ☐ _____
- ☐ _____
- ☐ _____
- ☐ _____
- ☐ _____
- ☐ _____
- ☐ _____
- ☐ _____
- ☐ _____
- ☐ _____
- ☐ _____
- ☐ _____
- ☐ _____
- ☐ _____
- ☐ _____

FRIDAY

SATURDAY

SUNDAY

"The music is not in the notes,
but the silence in between."

— *W.A. Mozart*

Date:

Goals

☐ _____
☐ _____
☐ _____
☐ _____
☐ _____

Total Practice Time:
_____

Date:

Goals

☐ _____
☐ _____
☐ _____
☐ _____
☐ _____

Total Practice Time:
_____

Notes: _____
_____
_____
_____
_____
_____
_____

Notes: _____
_____
_____
_____
_____
_____
_____

Date: _____

Goals

- [ ] _____
- [ ] _____
- [ ] _____
- [ ] _____
- [ ] _____

Total Practice Time:

_____

Notes: _____

_____
_____
_____
_____
_____
_____
_____

Date: _____

Goals

- [ ] _____
- [ ] _____
- [ ] _____
- [ ] _____
- [ ] _____

Total Practice Time:

_____

Notes: _____

_____
_____
_____
_____
_____
_____
_____

"Why hurry over beautiful things?
Why not linger and enjoy them?"

— *Clara Schumann*

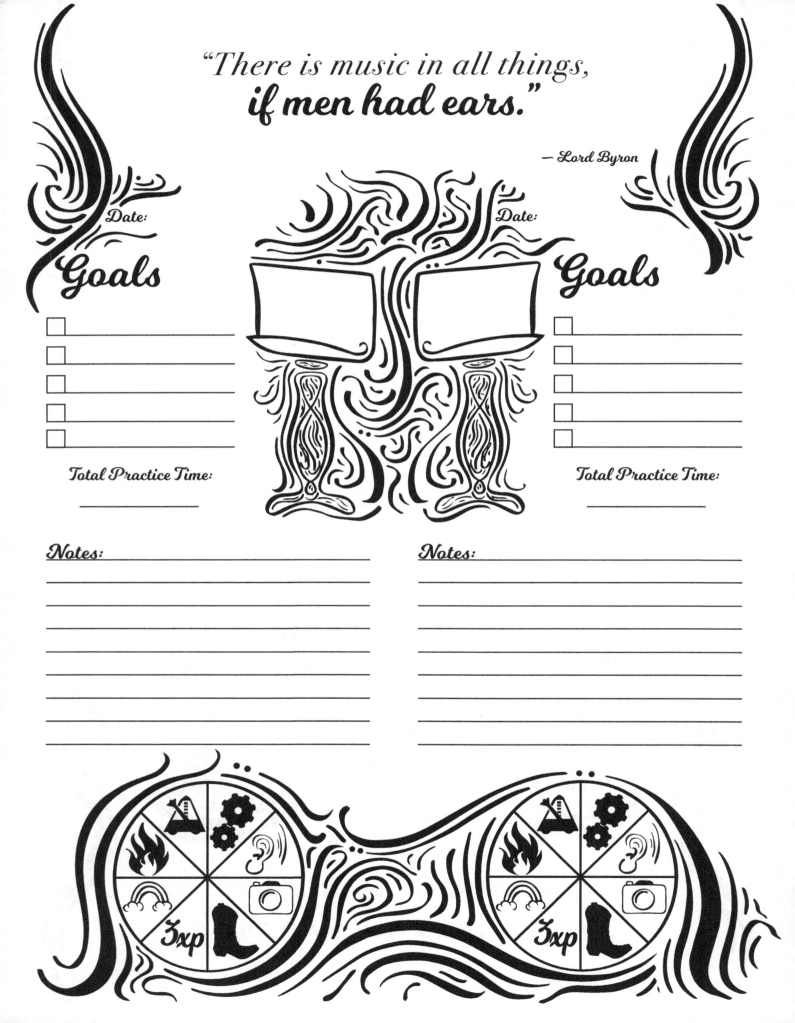

"*There is music in all things,*
if men had ears."

— *Lord Byron*

Date:

Goals

Total Practice Time:

Notes:

Date:

Goals

Total Practice Time:

Notes:

Rest Day

Lesson Notes:

_____
_____
_____
_____
_____
_____
_____
_____
_____
_____
_____
_____
_____
_____
_____
_____
_____
_____
_____
_____
_____
_____

Week In Review

What Went Well:

_____
_____
_____
_____
_____
_____

What I Can Do Better:

_____
_____
_____
_____
_____
_____
_____

Repertoire I Worked On This Week:

_____
_____
_____
_____

Don't forget to share your progress with your friends!

#PurposeIn Practice

Also Available on Amazon.com

Purpose In Practice
26 Rules for the Practicing Musician

At first glance, this volume is a practical handbook for effective practicing. But readers will quickly find that Purpose In Practice: 26 Goals for the Practicing Musician goes beyond the merely practical, into the truly meaningful. Indeed, this handbook provides a reading experience that is precisely as any practice session should be: practical yet dynamic, meticulous yet musical, focused yet enthralling. Rachel Lee Hall's top secrets for successful practice are here revealed in full, along with jewels of insight and advice from legendary musicians like Yolanda Kondonassis, Simone Dinnerstein, Richard Weiss, and others. At its heart, this book calls out to you, to abandon the endless monotony of ineffective routines, to instead seek out true meaning in your practice sessions—to practice with purpose—and so find great #PurposeInPractice.

Visit www.RachelLeeHall.com/books to learn more!

Follow Rachel on Social Media

 @RachelLeeHall   @RachelHallHarp   @RachelLeeHall

Made in the USA
Coppell, TX
09 March 2020